Touched

First directed by Richard Eyre at the Nottingham Playhouse in 1977, *Touched* was performed at the Royal Court Theatre, London, in 1981 and subsequently at regional theatres throughout Britain.

'The resonant public statements of the politicians are threaded through the ironic realism of life in a land fit for heroes flowing with milk and honey.'

Michael Coveney, *Financial Times*

Over one hundred days, the women in *Touched* celebrate the promise of a new world; Churchill broadcasts his messages of moral victory in the cause of freedom, there is talk of the soldier's return and an end to rationing. The Labour Party comes to power. The atom bomb forces peace with Japan. Stephen Lowe's magical play, first published in the Royal Court Writers' series and now in Methuen Modern Plays, is an intimate study of the lives of a group of Nottingham women testing the promise of a new world.

Stephen Lowe was born in 1947 in Nottingham. After graduating from Birmingham University in 1969, he spent six years writing, and doing a variety of jobs. While working as a shepherd in Yorkshire he was commissioned by Alan Ayckbourn and joined his company at Scarborough as an actor. His plays include *Comic Pictures* (Scarborough, 1976), *Sally Ann Hallelujah Band* (Nottingham Playhouse Theatre Roundabout, 1977), *Touched* (Nottingham Playhouse, 1977; Royal Court Theatre, 1981; joint winner of the George Devine Award), *The Ragged Trousered Philanthropists* (Joint Stock Theatre Company, 1978; Half Moon, London, 1983), *Glasshouses* (Royal Court Theatre Upstairs, 1981), *Tibetan Inroads* (Royal Court, 1981), *Moving Pictures* (Royal Court Theatre, 1981), *Seachange* (Riverside Studios, 1984), *Keeping Body and Soul Together* (Royal Court Theatre Upstairs, 1984), *Divine Gossip* (Royal Shakespeare Company's The Pit, Barbican Centre, 1988), and two television plays, *Shades* and *Cries from a Watchtower*. He has also edited a volume of *Peace Plays* for Methuen.

by the same author

DIVINE GOSSIP & TIBETAN INROADS

MOVING PICTURES – FOUR PLAYS
(Moving Pictures, Seachange, Stars, Strive)

PEACE PLAYS (Stephen Lowe, ed.)
(The Fence, Common Ground; *The Celebration of Kokura,* Berta
Freistadt; *Clam,* Deborah Levy; *Keeping Body and Soul Together,*
Stephen Lowe; *The Tragedy of King Real,* Adrian Mitchell)

THE RAGGED TROUSERED PHILANTHROPISTS

Stephen Lowe

Touched

METHUEN DRAMA

A METHUEN MODERN PLAY

First published in 1979 by Woodhouse Books, 12 Oldroyd,
Todmorden, Lancs.
Revised editon published in 1981 by Eyre Methuen Ltd,
in association with the Royal Court Theatre, Sloane Square,
London SW1.
Reprinted in 1981
Reprinted 1983, 1984 By Methuen London Ltd
Reprinted 1988 by Methuen Drama, Michelin House,
81 Fulham Road, London SW3 6RB and distributed in the
United States by HEB Inc, 70 Court Street, Portsmouth,
New Hampshire 03801.

British Library Cataloguing in Publication Data
Lowe, Stephen, *1947*
  Touched – Rev.ed – (Methuen modern plays)
  I. Title
  822'.914

    ISBN 0-413-61210-4

Printed in Great Britain by Expression Printers Ltd,
39 North Road, London N7 9DP

To my mother

Author's Note

I was not born until the Second World War had been over for two years. I was part of that post-war boom, the 'babies boom', bred out of joy, love, relief, accident or simply the resumption of old habits. And I grew up with the usual pulp of heroic war films, and comics, only much later challenged by a purge of anti-war literature. While I therefore gained a fairly graphic picture of the life of the soldier, it occurred to me, one fine day while talking with my mother, that I had hardly any picture of the world of those who stayed at home – those whose different battles had been fought in the landscape I had grown up in. I knew nothing, really, about the sacrifice and suffering of the women who only a few years later were to pick me up and put me down, and place pennies in my hand. Pennies I had never thought to return.

As I listened more closely to the tale of my mother and her friends, the background of this play about three sisters began slowly to grow, and as it grew, it focused on that 'stillpoint of the turning world', that time of peace that was not a full peace, war that was not a full war, that period where people hesitantly began to think they could risk breathing and hoping again – those one hundred days of summer from Victory in Europe Day in May, to Victory in Japan Day. I was considerably helped in understanding the wider ambiguities of this time by Angus Calder's remarkable work, *The People's War* – a time in which the impossible occurred; the impossible in horror seen at Belsen and overlooked at the time at Hiroshima, the impossible at home with the overthrow of Churchill and the arrival of a new Labour Government, the impossible in science with the splitting of the unsplittable atom – all encapsulated between Victory in Europe and Victory in Japan, and the coming of the final peace that many times must have seemed even more improbable.

Touched was first performed at the Nottingham Playhouse on 9 June, 1977, with the following cast:

SANDRA	Marjorie Yates
MARY	Lorraine Peters
BETTY	Kay Adshead
JOHNNY	Mick Ford
JOAN	Susan Tracy
PAULINE	Donna Owens/Seanna Watkinson
BRIDIE	Annie Hayes
KEITH	Malcolm Storry
HARRY	Brian Glover
MOTHER	Kristine Howarth

Directed by Richard Eyre
Designed by William Dudley
Lighting by Rory Dempster

Touched was performed at the Royal Court Theatre, London on 20 January, 1981, with the following cast:

SANDRA	Marjorie Yates
JOAN	Sharon Duce
BETTY	Kathryn Pogson
MOTHER	Elizabeth Bradley
PAULINE	Karen Dawson/Nicola Bullars
MARY	Jean Boht
BRIDIE	Anna Keaveney
KEITH	Ian Jentle
HARRY	Bill Dean
JOHNNY	Mike Packer

Directed by William Gaskill
Designed by Frank Conway
Lighting by Andy Phillips
Sound by Mic Pool

Characters

SANDRA
JOAN *her sister*
BETTY *their half-sister*
MOTHER
PAULINE *Joan's daughter*
MARY *a neighbour*
KEITH *a foreman*
BRIDIE *a friend*
HARRY *a chef*
JOHNNY

The play is set in and around Sneinton, Nottingham during the hundred day period from victory in Europe (VE) day, May 8, 1945 to victory in Japan (VJ) day, August 15,1945.

Scenes

1. The back of three terrace houses.
2. SANDRA'S living-room.
3. An hotel kitchen.
4. A part of Boots factory.
5. A clearing in the woods.
6. The top of Colwick woods

Lighting is crucial to the production. The set should be as simple as possible.

Note: All recordings are taken from either: *The Summer of 45*. A scrapbook of a momentous period. BBC52: or BBC1922.72. BBC Record 2 50B.

'No more my father's altar, but instead
The block of execution, reeking red
With blood my sacrifice shall shed.' *

Aeschylus: The Agamemnon

The Historical Background

The Eve of Peace

June 6, 1944
The D-Day landing by the Allies in Normany

August 1
Warsaw uprising

December 16
Battle of the Bulge

January 22, 1945
Burma road opened

March 16
Iwo Jima falls

April 1
U.S. landing on Okinawa

April 12
Roosevelt dies. Truman becomes President

April 13
Belsen and Buchenwald camps taken by British

April 16
Russian offensive towards Berlin

April 28
Mussolini killed

April 29
7th Army liberate Dachau

April 30
Hitler commits suicide

May 2
Red Army in Berlin

May 3
Allies capture Rangoon

The Hundred Days

May 8, 1945
VICTORY-IN-EUROPE (VE) DAY
Official announcement by Premier Churchill at 3.00pm

May 10
British fleet attacks Japanese near Formosa

May 13
Russians overcome resistance in Czechoslovakia

June 4
Churchill's opening election campaign speech. Labour manifesto entitled 'LET US FACE THE FUTURE' released

June 21
Okinawa falls to U.S.

June 26
United Nations established in San Francisco to 'save generations from the scourge of war'

July 5
POLLING DAY
Owing to army ballots, results will not be known until three weeks later

July 26
ELECTION RESULTS
Labour 'landslide'

July 27
Attlee becomes Prime Minister. The Allies at the Potsdam Conference 'reaffirm their intention to bring major war criminals to swift and sure justice'

August 6
First atomic bomb dropped on Hiroshima: 'a mushroom cloud $7\frac{1}{2}$ miles high'. Bank Holiday Monday

August 9
Russia declares war against Japan and invades Manchuria

August 10
Second atomic bomb on Nagasaki

August 14
Just before midnight Attlee's announcement of the end of the war

August 15
VICTORY IN JAPAN (VJ) DAY

Scene One

*The backyards of three terraced houses. Darkness. Yiddish Lament
'Kaddish der Jud ist rejodt' sung by a woman can be heard.*

RECORDING. (Richard Dimbleby): And here, over an acre of
ground, lay dead and dying people. You could not see which was
which except perhaps by a convulsive movement, or the last
quiver of a sigh from a living skeleton, too weak to move. The
living lay with their heads against the corpses, and around them
moved the ghastly procession of emaciated, aimless people, with
nothing to do, and no hope of life, unable to move out of your
way, unable to look at the terrible sights around them. There
was no privacy – nor did men and women ask it any longer.
Women stood and squatted stark naked in the dust trying to
wash themselves, and to catch the lice on their bodies.

*Under speech, slow light up on SANDRA, who stands facing the
audience holding a bundle of linen, perhaps a child. She is thin, and
dressed in dark, only adequate clothing.*

RECORDING. Babies had been born here, tiny wizened things
that could not live. A mother, driven mad, screamed at a British
sentry to give her milk for her child, and thrust the tiny mite
into his arms and ran off, crying terribly. He opened the bundle,
and found the baby had been dead for days. This day at Belsen
was the most horrible day of my life.

PROJECTION: Day 1. May 8, 1945. Victory-in-Europe Day.

SANDRA *remains. Under MARY's speech, slow light up on centre
stage. Sheets and clothing are hung up on an intricate patterning of
clothes-lines. There is a slight breeze. Full stage lighting.*

MARY (*hidden by washing*). We know it's over. Why coun't they
tell us yesterday? Oh, they never gi' ought away free, that lot,
not even Victory. Like to have you queue up and gi' thanks. We
don't know they'll tell us today. Waitin' for them to tell you
ought, you'd end up black as the hobs. It were a lovely drying
breeze yesterday. Even my Ted said get 'em out while it's
blowing. (*Silence.*) Thirty odd years and I've never held me
washing over from Monday to Tuesday. And it grieves me more
than ought. Still, they're drying a treat. (*Silence.*) Not that they
woun't have dried a treat yesterday.

MARY *appears from behind the washing; a woman in her late fifties.*

Yo' listenin'?

SANDRA. Wha'?

SANDRA *begins to fold her armful of linen.*

MARY. I said not that they woun't have dried yesterday.

SANDRA. I told you, Mary. I said they woun't tell us. Woun't 'ave it though, would you?

MARY. Din't see your washin' out yesterday.

SANDRA. Stuck wi'out your soapy water to get me copperload started off.

MARY (*laughing*). Had to muck in, an't we, Sandra?

SANDRA. Muck is right.

MARY. Lend a hand wi' me sheets, duck.

SANDRA *puts down her pile and crosses to help* MARY. MARY *ducks under a blanket.*

MARY. I don't know what you're doin', washing your blanket now.

SANDRA. What?

MARY. My mum used to say, 'Wash a blanket in May, Sure to wash somebody away'. (*Silence.*) Did they put that new one by for you?

SANDRA. Sorry?

MARY. At Whitings. Your new blanket.

SANDRA. Called in yesterday. Bit of good stuff. It'll last.

MARY. A good blanket should see you straight for life. Instead of this tat. (*Indicates the blanket.*) I don't know how you've stuck this winter. I could strain me peas through this. It's that threadbare.

SANDRA. I don't feel the cold much.

MARY. Just shiver for fun, I know. Whatever got into your head to gi' them good un's away from off your little un's bed?

SANDRA. No good to me. Cut down, anyroad. I can hardly see

me sister's kid goin' down wi' pneumonia.

MARY. Don't you go bein' too generous. There's some who'll take advantage. You spend more time looking after Pauline than Joan does, as it is.

SANDRA. I'll have paid up on the new one by September. Be all right while the summer's here.

They are folding the sheets.

MARY. Nice of them to put it on one side for you.

SANDRA. I'm payin' top for it.

MARY (*not listening*). Why don't they tell us? 'Stead of muckin' about. Al the world knows 'cept us.

SANDRA. Not long now.

MARY. Joan'll hear it, will she?

SANDRA. She's wired up to it, like a walking bomb.

MARY. She's a card, that one. You could do wi' a touch of her. You keep a sight too tight a rein on yourself.

SANDRA. Ye', well now summer's here I'll let me hair down a bit. Come on, sun, warm us up. That's lovely. Keep that up. I'm comin' alive now. When they gi' out the news I reckon I'll rip off all me clothes, and do the Highland Fling. How's that for starters?

MARY. Better lock me little hubby up then. Woun't want him overexcited. He gets faint if I so much as wave mistletoe near him at Christmas.

SANDRA. Our Joan would, if she were egged on. Ought for a laugh, her. Mind you, wi' me, there woun't be much to see.

MARY. Lean years.

SANDRA. Jack Spratt would eat no fat, his wife would eat no lean. Fancy having the choice, eh?

MARY. Be different now, though.

SANDRA. Will it?

MARY. Bound to be.

SANDRA. Why?

MARY. Spoils of Victory. Land of Milk and Honey. Even smiling Ted says that much.

SANDRA. I don't know.

MARY. Bound to be suspicious. All them false starts. But, honest, this is it. Look, the sun's out here, but I bet it's pissing down on Berlin. It's a sign is that.

SANDRA. Come on, sun. Burn the ice out of us. A Mediterranean tan would be nice.

MARY. Bet it's snowing in Italy. Them buggers'll never have no sun no more.

SANDRA. I woun't wish snow on 'em. Sick to death of blacks and whites. (*Quietly*:) Some colour, eh? Come on, sun.

MARY. You all right?

SANDRA. Bit on edge with it all, that's all.

MARY. Bound to be. (*Pause.*) Churchill'll tell us at three, will he?

SANDRA. He'll tell us at three.

MARY. Send you a telegram, did he?

SANDRA. Someat like that.

MARY. Do you want a fag?

SANDRA. No. Not long now. Let's hang on, and bring in the new world with a delicious Player's Weight. I've bin hoarding five special.

MARY. Bet your Joan's stocked up wi' Lucky Strikes.

SANDRA. Not right. A good Nottingham cigarette for good Nottingham gals.

There are now only a few sheets left.

MARY. Some of these are still a bit damp.

SANDRA. I wonder where Pauline is?

MARY. Stop fussing.

SANDRA. No, but it'd be nice if she's home with her mam for the news, woun't it?

MARY. Let Joan look after her a bit.

SANDRA. I don't mind.

MARY. Listen, luv, don't think me heartless. But there'll be plenty more, you know. When your Albert gets back, you'll find your hands full of nappies. That's how it was after the first war.

SANDRA. Oh, ye', there'll be others.

MARY. Not healthy harping on it. You're still young.

SANDRA. Was when the war started. Thirty-three now.

MARY. And you've kept yourself straight. Not like some I could name. You'll get your due now. Just wait and see. I'm an old woman and I'm telling you.

SANDRA. Where's me mam? Think she'd be here, woun't you?

MARY. She'll come.

SANDRA. All the family together. That *can* be together. That should be the way. Instead of off to find a glass of mild.

MARY. She's never.

SANDRA. It in't on, you know. It really in't.

MARY. Here's your Betty.

MARY *folds pillowcases etc.*

BETTY *is an attractive girl of seventeen. Slim, by no means a common beauty, she carries herself well. She's followed by* JOHNNY, *the same age, a clerk.*

MARY. Now then, Betty.

BETTY. Hello, Mrs Ellis, how are you?

SANDRA. An't you brought mam wi' you? Whole family should be together time like this.

BETTY. She's seeing somebody.

SANDRA. Who?

JOHNNY. Mrs Ellis.

MARY. Johnny.

BETTY (*quietly*). Who do you think?

SANDRA. Ye', well, he in't family.

BETTY. He is to me.

SANDRA. No, he in't. Not proper. Could have been. Could have been a dad to us all.

BETTY. T'in't his fault. It's her.

SANDRA. All this secret stuff. Keeping up appearances. Yo' can't even call him dad.

BETTY. Shurrup.

SANDRA. She should be here.

BETTY. We don't even know it's going to be now for definite.

SANDRA. I'll bet you any money.

BETTY. I had a hell of a job getting off. My shift din't work out like yours, you know.

SANDRA. You don't want to hear it at work. You want to hear it with your family. Them nearest to you.

MARY. How's things down at Raleigh, Johnny?

JOHNNY. Not half bad. Getting into the swing now.

SANDRA. What's he doing here?

MARY. Takes a bit of time.

JOHNNY. Yes.

BETTY. Mary had a little lamb. Its fleece was white as snow. And everywhere that Mary went, that lamb was sure to go.

JOHNNY *and* MARY *stop, and stare at her. She curtsies.*

SANDRA. You got *your* party piece, Johnny?

JOHNNY. I din't know . . . Nobody said . . .

MARY. They're pulling your leg, duck.

JOHNNY. Oh, ye'.

SANDRA. Now, let's get ourselves sorted. Sit out here to hear the news. Get a bit of sun. Specially on your pasty face. Moping about.

BETTY. I don't see why it's a joke when it happens to me. I don't see that, Sandra.

SANDRA. Johnny, do us a favour and move them sheets up a bit. Out of the way.

JOHNNY. Right.

MARY (to BETTY). They want the best for you. That's all.

BETTY. I know what they want. Just keep mum and suck the dummy.

SANDRA (calling into the house). Joan!

JOAN (voice). Hello?

SANDRA. Can you feed it through the window?

JOAN. I can stick it up the chimney if you want!

SANDRA. No, have you got enough wire?

JOAN. Plenty.

SANDRA. Pass it through.

JOAN. Hang on.

BETTY. Honest. It's bad enough having to drag him around.

MARY. Why, he's practically part of the family.

BETTY. As close as he comes.

MARY. He's harmless.

BETTY. He's such a baby. I know he can't help it, but he should be out there fighting. And when you've lost your love you can't do with kids kicking about your heels.

SANDRA (*calling to* JOHNNY). Don't drag them in the dirt. I've just washed them.

JOHNNY. Right. (*He is desperately trying to manage a whole unfolded sheet.*)

BETTY. Look at that. Here. (*She crosses to him.*)

JOHNNY. Thank you, Betty.

MARY. I'll nip and get some chairs.

SANDRA. Get a move on. Not long now.

MARY enters her back-door. SANDRA takes the wireless through the open window, and tries to make it to the dustbin, but the lead does not quite stretch that far.

SANDRA. Move this dustbin up, Johnny.

JOHNNY. Oh, ye'.

SANDRA. Might as well make yourself useful.

JOHNNY. Sure thing.

JOAN enters. Mid-twenties, a live wire, tending to the bonny side. Well made-up.

JOAN. Sure thing, pardner. (*She mimes a shoot-out with* JOHNNY. *Laughs.*) Hi, handsome! Oh, Betty, be a love, and bring the tea-things out. We'll have a picnic.

BETTY. You've got legs, haven't you?

JOAN. I have but they're not for walking on. Go on, luv, do us a favour.

BETTY enters the house.

SANDRA. I can't get ought on this.

JOAN. Let's have a go.

She crosses to the radio. MARY appears, piling chairs outside her door. JOHNNY carries them over and places them around the dustbin. SANDRA carefully positions them. BETTY enters with tea-things.

BETTY. Where?

SANDRA. Put them down there. (*Indicating by* SANDRA'*s chair.*)

BETTY *sits, dejected, on the edge of the wall.*

JOAN. Little bugger. It was right as rain in there.

SANDRA. It had better go.

MARY. Should I get mine?

JOAN. It'll go. I'm marvellous with knobs.

SANDRA. Now then, Joan!

JOAN. Just slipped out. (*Laughs. Blows* JOHNNY *a kiss.*)

MARY. Tea, and all. In't it cosy?

JOAN. Would you care to be mother, Betty?

BETTY. Very funny.

JOAN. Johnny would give you a hand.

JOHNNY. Oh ye'!

SANDRA. I'll pour.

She begins to do so. JOHNNY *attempts to pass the tea out.* MARY *sits on a chair.*

SANDRA. Don't sit there, Betty, or you will catch something to make you as miserable as you look.

BETTY (*rising*). It's all right for you. Your men are coming back.

JOAN. Vivien Leigh!

BETTY. I'm not talking to you.

She sits down on a chair. Pause. Some static from the radio.

SANDRA. Sit down, Johnny.

JOHNNY *sits down.*

Your tea's by your chair, Joan.

Quiet, apart from the static.

MARY. In't this posh?

JOAN. Got him. Blood-Sweat-and-Tears himself!

SANDRA. Turn it up.

JOAN. Right. (*She turns it up.*)

RADIO. Are you sitting comfortable, then I'll begin.

JOAN. Gi' it to us straight, Winnie.

RADIO. Today I am going to tell you the story of three little pigs –

SANDRA. Turn it down.

JOAN (*impersonating Churchill*): Today . . . I am going to tell you . . . the story of three little pigs . . . and how they fought the big bad wolf on the beaches and in the fields and on the streets . . .

SANDRA. Turn it right down.

JOAN. That's the way to end a crazy war. Listen with Mother.

She turns it down, but occasionally, in the pause, a reference to the little pigs can be heard enough to make JOAN *or* JOHNNY *giggle. Even* BETTY *is smiling.*

JOAN. Nice to see you smiling, for a change.

BETTY *stops smiling.*

Sorry I spoke, I'm sure.

A restless silence reigns. Eventually, JOAN *rises to pour herself a second cup.*

Top up, anybody?

BETTY *passes her cup across.* JOAN, *about to pour, takes a deep interest in the tea-leaves at the bottom of the cup.*

Hello, hello, hello, what have we here?

BETTY. Always have to put your spoke in.

JOAN. Well, I'll go to the foot of our stairs. If that isn't a . . . by Jove, he's a big lad . . . good-looking fellow. Well, I say that. I

can't see his face, but by the rest of him he ain't half bad . . .
well, I never did. Not that you have yet, but you soon will.

JOHNNY. What do you see?

BETTY. Take no notice. Anyway, you don't read tea leaves like
that, do you, Sandra?

SANDRA. What?

BETTY. You don't read tea-leaves like that, do you?

SANDRA. Sorry. Miles away then. Er, no, she's having you on.

JOAN. OK, clever, you show us. (*Passes* SANDRA *the cup.*)

BETTY. Go on, Sandra.

SANDRA. I don't know how to do it. Not really. Granma Granger
was always playing at it, when I used to run her errands. Used to
watch her sometimes.

JOHNNY. What do you see in there?

SANDRA. Tea-leaves.

BETTY. Oh, come on Sand. Just to pass the time.

SANDRA. Ought for peace and quiet. Swill the cup round three
times, that's it, and turn it over into the saucer. Now, pass it
here.

JOHNNY. Will you do mine, afterwards?

SANDRA. It's only a game.

BETTY. Hush. She has to go into a trance.

JOAN (*singing*). That old black magic has me in its spell . . .

SANDRA. Silence, please. Oh ye', it's coming now. Yes, strange
forms are floating in front of my eyes.

JOHNNY. Told you. That's what I saw. Strange forms.

BETTY. Ssssh! (*Leans over to turn the radio down.*)

SANDRA. Don't turn that off, Betty. We don't want to miss it.

MARY. I'll keep an ear out.

BETTY. Now, Sand, what do you see?

SANDRA. It's coming clearer now. Like a snowstorm settling. I see a tall, dark and handsome man.

JOAN. She's going to marry a blackie. That'll please our mam.

SANDRA. He's not black, but he has fine black hair. And you're going to meet him very soon. He's not English, but there's a bit of class to him. And he'll dance you away into your dreams.

JOAN. I hope he's got a bob or two.

MARY. Don't be so unromantic, Joan.

BETTY. I know it's only a game. No-one's going to dance me away.

JOAN. Cheerful little sod.

SANDRA. And he'll take you away, far away, across the waters.

JOHNNY. Eh, you'll go and live in West Bridgford. You'll love that. Bread and Lard Island.

SANDRA. Far away to his home across the waters – to a huge house wi' tons of room. Surrounded by water, as well.

JOHNNY. A castle?

JOAN. Alcatraz! It's Al Capone. A bloody I-tie.

SANDRA. It could be a castle.

BETTY. To go abroad, and live in a castle.

JOAN. Or even a council house.

JOHNNY. What happens next?

SANDRA. Nothing. They live happily ever after, as in all the best stories.

She leans over to turn up the radio. Music.

JOHNNY. Did you see someat, really?

BETTY. Course she did, stupid. What she said. When will I meet him?

JOAN. You're as daft as a brush, the pair of you.

BETTY (*defiantly*). Why? Somebody's got to meet princes. Why not me?

JOAN. Well, of course, there's hundreds of princes down the Palais every Friday –

SANDRA. Shut up a minute. They're saying someat.

She reaches towards the radio.
Momentary blackout. The scene lit, with overhead spot, on the radio.
The actors freeze.

RECORDING ANNOUNCER. The Prime Minister. The Rt. Hon. Winston Churchill.

CHURCHILL. Yesterday morning at 2.41 am at General Eisenhower's headquarters, General Jodl, the representative of the German High Command, and the Grand-Admiral Doenitz, the designated head of the German state, signed the act of unconditional surrender of all German Land, Sea and Air Forces in Europe.

Followed by the cease fire.

Blackout.

Lighting as before. The group sit, silent, unmoving.

SANDRA. It's over.

JOAN. All bar the shouting.

SANDRA. I don't believe it. (*Head down.*)

JOAN. Now then, duck.

BETTY. What do you say?

Silence. Eventually –

JOAN. Lighting up time.

SANDRA. Here, I saved these special.

She gives cigarettes to MARY and JOAN.

JOHNNY. Can I have one?

SANDRA. Course you can.

JOAN. Starting bad habits, eh?

They light up. BETTY *begins to cry quietly.*

SANDRA (*passing her hanky, gently*). And you without a hanky.
Little Miss Proper. Slipping up.

JOAN. First fag of freedom.

MARY. I were gasping.

*Silence. They watch the smoke rise. Bells begin to peal, followed by
sirens, horns, shouting.*

MARY. Listen to them bells. Dreaded them of a night. In case
they'd come. But it's a noise worth hearing, now.

JOAN. Come on, then, let us make some noise. We'll show them
buggers we're not dead yet. (*She stands behind the radio.*)

JOAN (*as Regimental Sergeant-Major*). Come on, on your feet you
dead and alive horrible little squirts. Let's hear your voices for
Britannia! Come on. Achtung. Achtung. Sieg Heil! Sieg Heil!

They rise.

Burn you bastards, burn in hell. You thought you'd done for us.
All bar the shouting. Well, you'll hear us shouting now. Let's
hear you, you grubby little buggers, let's hear you sing the song
that has held England together through its darkest hour. After
me in dulcet tones.

She begins to sing, to the amusement of the others.

Hitler, he's only got one ball.
Goering has two but very small.
Himmler is somewhat similiar.
And poor old Goebbels has no balls at all!

SANDRA. Now then, Joan. Kids present (*Laughing.*)

JOHNNY *has joined in enthusiastically.*

JOAN. On the drums, Johnny.

JOHNNY. The what?

JOAN (*throwing him a dustbin lid*). Get banging. Betty, get us some music, me and Mary'll show you how to dance.

She passes the radio to BETTY *who tunes in to a Victor Sylvester style version of 'Down Mexico Way';* JOHNNY *begins to bash the dustbin lid.*
JOAN *drags* MARY *into a 'dance'.* JOHNNY, *finding a second dustbin lid, beats out a Congo, which all, bar* BETTY, *join in. It breaks up in chaos.* JOHNNY *going one way, the women another.*

JOAN. Die, you bastards, die. (*Getting her breath back.*) Right, come on. Let's get on the town before the booze all goes.

MARY. Better get meself spruced up for Ted coming back.

JOAN. Don't tire him out, duck. It's going to be a long day.

MARY. See you in the best room down the Dale.

She goes.

BETTY. I'd better go and find me mam.

JOAN. Don't you go sloping off til you've got your marching orders. It's time you bucked your ideas up, me lady. Look, luv, he was a pen-pal, a nice lad, not Robert Taylor, but he was all right. You met him once, and then he went down on his ship. Sad, but it happened. Thousands went down like that. But now it's over. Finished. And you've got to forget.

BETTY. It's easy for you to talk.

JOAN. Forget it. Now I'm telling you. I'm not having you buggering up my celebrations, wi' blokes endlessly asking where that mardy-arsed, but beautiful sister of mine has got to, so –

BETTY. Just leave off, Joan, will you?

JOAN. No chance. Now nip home and get into someat with a bit of colour, and me and Sand'll come and collect you and Mam. And while you're at it, them letters that you've got tied up in a ribbon in your handbag –

BETTY. How do you know about them?

JOAN. I'm your sister. There in't much I don't know about you. Take 'em out and burn 'em in the grate.

BETTY. You're callous, You know that?

JOAN. Don't muck me about, duck. I want to show you off a bit. Johnny, take close guard of her.

JOHNNY. Right.

BETTY. I'll come, Joan. But don't ask me to like it.

JOAN. You're too kind. Now get off and tell our Mam to get dolled up, an' all.

BETTY (*going*). I don't need you, Johnny.

She goes.

JOAN. If you lose her, you'll have me to reckon with.

JOHNNY. I'll keep an eye on her.

He goes. JOAN *unpins a Union Jack.*

JOAN (*turning*). I'd better pin summat together for our Pauline when she gets back. Victory parades and the like. And I'll rip them bloody black-outs down an' all.

She turns to face SANDRA. *They stand, quietly, some distance apart.* SANDRA *is crying.*

JOAN. You're entitled.

SANDRA. Be all right. (*She smiles.*)

JOAN. Rainbow through the tears. (*Pause.*) Get your glad rags on, make you feel better. Wear that white lace-edged dress. You look lovely in that.

SANDRA. I'll just take the washing in.

JOAN. Bugger the washing. Bugger the world.

SANDRA. I can't do that.

JOAN. You have to learn. (*Silence.*) Our Pauline takes after you. Washes up, all dainty like. Old-fashioned kid. Come on. Snap out of it. Five minutes, right.

SANDRA. Five minutes.

JOAN *enters her house.* SANDRA *reaches up and grasps one of the lines. She freezes looking out over the audience. As the lights fade the noise from the street builds, merging in with the crowd noises of the next recording.*

RECORDING. ANNOUNCER. And now, oh what wonderful luck, at this moment, how wonderful, Mr Churchill has come out onto the Ministry of Health's balcony.

Slow spot up on an eight-year-old child, PAULINE. *She wears a pinned up 'tunic' of the Union Jack, with a pillow stuffed under it; an old suit jacket, and a black saucepan on her head. She smokes a mock cigar, and holds a card with '1st' on it.*

ANNOUNCER. He's wearing his boiler suit, the famous boiler suit he has made so wonderful, and he's putting on his black hat, nobody can say that it goes with the boiler suit but you heard what a cheer it raised from the crowd. And he stands in the floodlight and he's giving his Victory sign, with all his might from the floodlit balcony.

PAULINE *makes a victory sign, and giggles. She slowly begins to revolve, almost dancing in a tired fashion.*

CHURCHILL. This is your Victory. Victory of the Cause of Freedom in every land. In all our long history we have never seen a greater day than this. Everyone, every man and woman, have done their bit, everyone has tried, none have scrimped, in the long years and the dangers, or the fierce attack of the enemy, have in no way weakened the unbending resolve of the British nation. God Bless you ALL!

ANNOUNCER. And now, listen. The band is playing Land of Hope and Glory, and the crowd is singing, and this suddenly has become a very moving moment. For Mr Churchill is singing, and he is conducting the singing of the song. Will you listen, please?

Sudden silence.

PAULINE (*softly*). Land of Hope and Glory
Mother of the free . . . (*Pause.*)
God who made thee might . . . er . . .
Make thee . . .

She can remember no more. She's very tired. Slow fade.

Scene Two

The scene as before. Night. The curtains of SANDRA's *house have been taken down, and the dark yards are now lit in elongated patches by the light from hers and the houses opposite. Occasionally the sound and colours of fireworks illuminate the stage. Sounds of party from* JOAN's *house. At the edge of hearing Glen Miller's version of 'Don't Fence Me In'.* SANDRA *leaves* JOAN's *house and enters her own. She appears on her step.*

SANDRA. Pauline, Pauline! Where are you?

She crosses down-stage to the darkened lavatory.

Anyone in there?

Silence. She listens.

Pauline, are you in there?

PAULINE (*off*). Yes, Auntie Sandra.

SANDRA. What are you doing?

PAULINE (*off*). Listening to the music.

SANDRA. Come on. You're s'posed to be tucked up in bed. Out. No mucking about.

PAULINE *comes out.*

SANDRA. Well, you do look a sorry sight, and no mistake.

PAULINE. Can I go to the party?

SANDRA. You've had your party for today. You can hardly stand up you're that tired. Anyhow, it's not a proper party. No jelly, or ought. Not too keen on it meself.

PAULINE. I put me party dress back on.

SANDRA. So I see.

PAULINE. I won.

SANDRA. Your mam's ever so proud. She's telling everybody about you.

PAULINE. Is she?

SANDRA. Well, if you don't fancy bed, come keep me company a bit, eh? What have you got up here – kittens?

She removes the pillow padding.

Sit on that. It'll take the cold off your bum.

They sit in the dark.

PAULINE. What you doing?

SANDRA. Lighting a fag.

PAULINE. Light mine as well. (*Holds up cigar.*)

SANDRA. You save that one. Special.

PAULINE. Do you think me mam'll let me have a pet now?

SANDRA. She might. You never know.

PAULINE. Are you going to have a pet?

SANDRA. I'm going to have more than a pet. I'm going to have hundreds of animals. Lots of cows and sheep.

PAULINE. Round here?

SANDRA. No, not round here. I'm going to join one of them Wagon Trains, and go out West. And soon I'll be sitting up on high, with a pretty little bonnet on, and my dress all swelled out with petticoats, bouncing across the Prairies. Jess by my side, a quiet, strong man, a man a woman could be proud of.

PAULINE. Where's Uncle Albert?

SANDRA. Do you remember your Uncle Albert?

PAULINE. Not really.

SANDRA. Remember your Dad?

PAULINE. Oh yes. Don't like him.

SANDRA. Why not?

PAULINE. Rows all the time.

SANDRA. Be different now.

PAULINE. Where will you live?

SANDRA. Just keep going 'til we come to the end of the rainbow.

PAULINE. What rainbow?

SANDRA. An't they told you the story about the rainbow at Sunday School?

PAULINE. Don't remember.

SANDRA. Oh, it's a smashing story . . . You see, God once thought men were so wicked that he'd start all over again, so he flooded the world and everybody got drowned. Everybody except Noah, who he had let in on it, and Noah put his family and loads of animals all in a big boat and they rode the storm out, and to show Noah that he wouldn't wipe men out again, he gave him a sign which was the rainbow. The rainbow is made by the sun coming out whilst it's still raining, you see. And you get all these colours like the fireworks, and you know everything's going to get better and the rain isn't going on for much longer, and then you follow that rainbow, and when you get to the end you find a pot of gold, and that's the promised land; California. And me and Jess will build this big house there, and have a huge family, and lots of animals, and work hard, and sing songs, and you can come and spend your holidays with us.

Another flare illuminates her face – the child is asleep. She puts out her cigarette. JOHNNY *coughs.*

SANDRA. Who's that?

JOHNNY (*stepping into the light*). Me. Johnny.

SANDRA. You shoun't go sneaking up on folk like that.

JOHNNY. I was trying not to make you jump. That's why I coughed. Only I walk light, I'm not very heavy.

SANDRA. I'm a bit nervy, that's all. Were just telling the kid a story.

JOHNNY. Yes.

SANDRA. What you up to then?

JOHNNY. I wondered if Betty were here.

SANDRA. She weren't in the party when I was there.

JOHNNY. Lost her up the arboretum. It's floodlit up there.

SANDRA. I saw they'd done Slab Square.

JOHNNY. And the castle. Just like the back of the fag packets. Would you care for a cigarette?

SANDRA. You've bought some, have you?

JOHNNY. Ye', I did.

SANDRA. Pop in. Have a look. She might have turned up.

JOHNNY. Might. Here you are.

SANDRA. I've just put one out, duck.

JOHNNY. Can treat yourself a bit now.

SANDRA. Go on then. Don't wake little un up, though.

He lights her cigarette, and begins to walk around.

JOHNNY. Much warmer now, in't it?

SANDRA. Ye'.

JOHNNY. Do you think she'll be all right?

SANDRA. She's got a head on her shoulders. She'll come to no harm tonight.

JOHNNY. I don't mind. I just keep her company, make sure she's all right.

SANDRA. Not a lot of mates left for you to knock around with, is there?

JOHNNY. Get used to it.

SANDRA. Do you still get your . . . you still have your fits, do you?

JOHNNY. Nought like I used to. I woun't be surprised if it disappeared completely. Mr Fowler who runs the warehouse says when we get a proper health system, they'll set me up in no time, and I'll be out there wi' the lads, gi'in' it the Japs.

SANDRA (*pauses*). Good.

JOHNNY. Where did they find Mr Downes?

SANDRA. One of them camps near Rangoon, somewhere.

JOHNNY. Be home soon, then, will he?

SANDRA. Telegram said they were sending him to Australia for six months. To recuperate. Doing that with all the POWs. I don't know that they won't send him back in the fight again. You never know what they'll do.

A really incandescent, irridescent firework.

JOHNNY. They must be shooting them off the castle.

SANDRA. The last time I remember the sky lit up like this, was '41 Summer. When they hit us. I was coming out of the house, with Jimmy, to get down the Anderson, just coming out the backdoor here, and he starts laughing. He'd be what, two, and we stood on this step and looked up at that sky. It didn't seem real after all that waiting for 'em, more like a film. Course it didn't have any meaning to Jimmy not at his age, but it didn't have a lot for me. It was just a fantastic night sky with these long white beams and flares of all colours, reds, blues, greens; the whole place lit up. Like a giant bonfire. Fires. Like tonight. And he was killing himself laughing, and reaching out to catch the flares, like night butterflies. Funny that he were safer then wi' all the lights and bombs, than in the blackout.

JOHNNY. Mr Fowler says there'll be an election soon. Get our people in this go. Labour Party. I'm going to canvas round here. For Mr Harrison, I think. They need people like me, he said.

SANDRA. Me arm's gone dead. I'd better get her up to my bed, 'fore she catches her death.

JOHNNY. Here. (*He laboriously picks the child up.*)

SANDRA. Don't drop her, for Christ's sake. Here. Give her me.

JOHNNY. You shouldn't be carrying her.

SANDRA. Why ever not?

JOHNNY. Well, you are a woman.

SANDRA (*smiles*). Out the road.

She enters the house with PAULINE. JOHNNY *stands outside,
watching the flares. He pretends to machine-gun an aeroplane.*
SANDRA *comes out of the house and crosses over to* JOAN's.

SANDRA. Still here?

JOHNNY. Did you really see ought in them tea-leaves?

SANDRA. Something. Pictures. Imagination.

JOHNNY. And did you see what you told her?

SANDRA. Something like. Are you comin' in?

JOHNNY. I get pictures, sometimes, when I have a turn.

SANDRA. Comin' in or staying out?

JOHNNY. Do you ever walk up top of Colwick Woods?

SANDRA. No, never. When would I get the time?

JOHNNY. I often go up there. I thought, if you ever –

SANDRA. Have you been drinking?

JOHNNY. I called in the Dale, but he said he'd ran out. He
always says that when I go in. You write to your husband and
tell him to vote for Labour Party.

SANDRA. You think it'll make a difference.

JOHNNY. Safe as houses. Bet you.

SANDRA. I don't have a lot to bet with, Johnny.

JOHNNY. I woun't say that . . .

SANDRA (*moving away*). Get along with you.

JOHNNY (*yelling*). Vote Labour and get the bastards out!

She enters the house. JOHNNY *crosses to the door, changes his mind
and peers through the window as the lights fade and . . .*

RECORDING. CHURCHILL. We may allow ourselves a brief
period of rejoicing but let us not forget for a moment the toils
and efforts that lie ahead. Japan with all her treachery and greed
remains unsubdued. The injuries she has inflicted upon Great
Britain, the United States and other countries, and her detestable

cruelties call for Justice and Retribution. We must now devote all our strength and resources to the completion of our task both at home and abroad. Advance Britannia. Long Live the Cause of Freedom. God Save the King!

Blackout.

PROJECTION: Day 59. July 5. Polling Day.

Scene Three

The factory. White light. White set. SANDRA, JOAN and a third girl, BRIDIE, are standing at a long bench, on which are three Bunsen-burners. The girls are soldering the ends of small injection-type capsules. On their right-hand side the open phials, on their left, collecting boxes, a jug and a tumbler full of blackcurrant juice. All three are dressed in white protective clothing.

KEITH TOMPKINS, *a man his mid-twenties, crosses the stage.* BRIDIE *and* JOAN, *mockingly, hold high their tumblers.*

KEITH. That's it, girls. Keep taking the blackcurrant juice. (*He goes.*)

BRIDIE. Leery little bogger.

JOAN. I can just about bear it with gin.

BRIDIE. I had heard that! (*Laughs, coughs.*) These fumes. It's a national disgrace.

JOAN. Be bloody gassed to death. I'll have him when he comes back. Supposed to be looking into this, the little arse licker.

BRIDIE. Joan! And you a lady!

JOAN. He's nowt less.

They resume work.

BRIDIE. You get out last night?

JOAN. Last half-hour in the Dale, that was all.

BRIDIE. Slippin' a bit.

JOAN. Well, our Pauline's having nightmares. Goes the whole war as good as gold and now she starts. Sleep walking an' all. The whole works. Very embarrassing is that.

BRIDIE. I can well see that.

JOAN. All I need, for her to climb in wi' me, and wet the bed, and that's an end of my American Aid.

BRIDIE. Don't look now, but Winnie's back.

KEITH *enters.*

JOAN. Nice day out there, is it? Your tan's coming on a treat.

He walks, past, intent on his clipboard.

BRIDIE. He's playing hard to get.

JOAN. No chance, and he knows it. Oy! Mr Tompkins! Sir!

KEITH. What is it now, Joan?

JOAN. Can I tell you something, Sir?

KEITH. Come on, Joan. Get your little joke over.

JOAN. No joke, Sir, I just wanted to offer your Highness a bit of advice. You know you're toadying to the wrong side, don't you?

BRIDIE. Ye', you should be creeping to us. 'Cos after this election we'll be running this shop. We'll have it nationalised before you've time to say Winston Churchill.

KEITH. That would be typical of you lot to knife the man who saved you in the back. Fortunately most people have –

JOAN. And the first thing we'll do is get rid of these fumes. We'll care about folk a bit.

KEITH. Now come on, Joan. I've told you a thousand times you'll be safe and sound as long as you keep drinking the blackcurrant.

JOAN. And, of course, we believe you, Keith. I mean, how can we not believe a man who got himself priority listing, so they can't ship him out, a man who can't stay ten minutes in here without rushing outside to get a lungful. Course we believe you all right.

KEITH. Joan, don't push your luck with me.

JOHNNY. Oh, gerroff.

KEITH. You take too many liberties wi' me.

JOAN (*laughing*). Still hoping are you?

KEITH (*embarrassed*). I'm sick of your endless aspersions –

JOAN. Aspersions! Christ! From the Bottoms to High Pavement!
A success story! Who do you think you're coming it wi'!

KEITH. I don't know what's got into you today, Joan, but I'm not
having anymore. Right? Now there's a war on, so –

BRIDIE. Back to the top-secret war work. Code-name STAG!

KEITH. So let's get to it. (*He turns away.*)

JOAN. You still reckon we don't know what we're about here,
don't ya?

KEITH. We don't recognise Union meetings. In your own time.
Right?

JOAN. You men are dirty boggers. All supposed to be out there,
fighting for King and Country, instead of which, they're
sweating away doubling the population of Germany in nine
months. And we gals have to stand on our feet all day, kidded
on by the likes of you, making these tubes to be jabbed in our
lads' arms so they can safely have another couple of rounds with
some Deutschland tart.

KEITH. Who told you that?

JOAN. He looks surprised. We have someat up here (*Taps her
head.*) as well, you know. We have brains enough to see what the
game is. And we'll make them fraternising sods pay when they
come back.

KEITH. I don't know how you've got the face to stand there, and
say that. I know a thing or two about you, Joan Stephens.

JOAN. And I know a thing or two about you, sonny Jim. I've seen
you put your hand in your pocket for the young gals in the Dog
and Bear. So don't come whiter than white wi' me. It won't
wash. 'Sides (*Laughing.*) what I've done I've done for the war
effort. Never let the lads down. That motto's been emblazoned

across my chest.

BRIDIE. Rule Britannia!

JOAN. I have never enjoyed it. No sound of pleasure has ever escaped my ruby lips.

BRIDIE. Bless you.

KEITH. And you're the one's going to sort her husband out when he gets home. I've never 'eard ought like it.

JOAN. There's a bit of difference in having a drink wi' the allies, and having it away with the enemy. I've never held truck with that, and I never will. I'm not one of those women who queue up on top of woods for the I-tie prisoners. That sickens me that does. Them women in France who had their heads shaved, got their due, but there shoun't be two laws, and our boys who go with the enemy are just as bad. Victory don't make it different.

KEITH. I look forward to seeing your husband with his hair shaved off.

JOAN. I'll shave a sight more off than that if he's been up to tricks. I don't mind allies – fair enough. Got to keep their morale up.

BRIDIE *giggles*.

But the enemy –

BRIDIE. Eh, your Sandra –

SANDRA *faints*.

JOAN. Catch her, 'fore she bangs her head.

KEITH *catches her*.

KEITH. What's the matter, duck? Are yo all right?

JOAN. Of course, she in't all right, you daft sod. Get off her.

KEITH. Give her some blackcurrant juice.

JOAN. How you feeling, luv?

SANDRA *mumbles, shakes her head*.

KEITH. Put her head between her legs.

JOAN. It's fresh air she wants, not gymnastics. I'll take her home.

KEITH. Yes, you'd better.

JOAN. Give us a hand to get her changed, Bridie. Come on luv, you'll soon be home.

KEITH. Tell her to take a couple of days off.

JOAN. It's you and your bloody fumes done this. I'm warning you, if ought happens to my sister I'm holding you personally responsible.

KEITH. She'll be all right.

JOAN (*going off with* SANDRA). She'd better be.

BRIDIE *stands for a moment looking at* KEITH.

KEITH. I'll prop a door open, when you come back.

BRIDIE. We'll all be out of this soon. Back down the lace market making top money.

She goes off. KEITH *turns off the Bunsen, sniffs, takes a drink of blackcurrant.*

Blackout.

RECORDING. VERA LYNN. I'd like to dedicate my song not to the boys in Europe but to those in the East. You are still very far from those you love and those who love you. You still have other battles to fight. But we are thinking of you, praying for you, and wishing you well.

Sings first two lines of 'I'll be seeing you'.

Lights up on –

Scene Four

SANDRA's *living room. A drop-leaf, circular dining table. Threadbare settee. Couple of dining chairs. A small room.*

SANDRA *is lying on the settee, covered by a blanket.* JOAN *is pouring her a drink.*

JOAN. This gin'll set you up. Mother's ruin from me little medical cabinet. Get that down you.

SANDRA. I don't . . . I just want to sleep.

JOAN. Doctor's orders. Do you want I should fetch you the Doctor?

SANDRA. No. No. I'm all right. Just a bit foggy. Can I have some air?

JOAN. Just drink that like a good girl, or I will get him.

SANDRA *drinks.*

You're shivering. You warm enough?

SANDRA. I'm getting a new blanket, for him coming home.

JOAN. But are you warm enough now, duck?

SANDRA. Boiling. Can you open the curtains?

JOAN. Best leave 'em shut for a bit.

SANDRA. Is it night time?

JOAN. Not yet.

SANDRA. What happened?

JOAN. I want to talk to you, Sandra. Here you are. (*She fills up her glass.*) You keep yourself to yourself far too much.

SANDRA. I'll have to go to bed. I feel queer.

JOAN. Just settle yourself, and sup up a mo'. While we have a chat.

SANDRA *giggles.*

Are you feeling a bit better?

SANDRA. I feel like I'm in a Scotch mist.

JOAN *moves a cushion to perch on the settee and reveals some comics hidden there.*

JOAN. What you doing, keeping these cowboy comics, Sandra?

SANDRA. I wanted to keep ahead of him. Seeing his Dad wasn't here. I wanted to keep ahead of him.

JOAN. You should get shot of them.

SANDRA. Some good stories in there.

JOAN. I'll clear them out for you.

SANDRA. Don't touch them!

JOAN. All right. It's all right. I'll not touch them.

SANDRA. Why can't we have a window open?

JOAN. The walls are thin enough.

SANDRA. And the curtain's closed.

JOAN. Did you hear me, Sandra, I said the walls are thin enough.

SANDRA. You can hear everything through them walls.

JOAN. I can hear you in the morning, luv, being sick. As plain as day. For the last couple of weeks.

SANDRA. Them fumes.

JOAN. Sandra, I'm your sister, love. It's me, Joan. You always were close, but even you can't hide this for ever. How far gone are you?

SANDRA. I don't want to talk about it.

JOAN. You've got to talk about it. How long?

SNDRA. Getting on for three month.

JOAN. What are you going to do?

SANDRA. Can I have a drink of water, please?

JOAN. Here. (*She pours her more gin.*) You can't have it duck, you know that, don't you? I mean, there's no way you can have it. Not with him coming back like that. I can understand how you feel, but there'll be others, and it'll be right then. They'll be his.

SANDRA. I want to sit up.

JOAN. Let me.

SANDRA. I can manage. Where's me bag?

JOAN. What you after?

SANDRA. I want a fag.

JOAN finds her bag.

JOAN. You're out.

SANDRA. I must have a fag.

JOAN. I'll pop next door and get some. Stay just there.

SANDRA. I'm not going anywhere.

JOAN. You'll have to get rid of it, luv. Can't have another man's child. Think of Albert. (*Pause.*) Back in a jiffy.

She goes out. SANDRA *sits, facing the audience, cup in hand.*

SANDRA. Push . . . Push . . . (*Flicks her hand.*) . . . Push . . . I push the cup towards him. Albert. Sitting there. Don't you turn. Don't you have to turn. Sugared, stirred. Save him turning. I don't want to see your face. Grunting with effort. Old man. Dirty man. Could have put your shirt on. Fight to get that vest off you. Shaming me. Albert. Dirty man. Old man. Push . . . Push . . . Push . . .

JOAN returns towards the end of the speech, with a lighted cigarette.

JOAN. Steady on, duck.

SANDRA. I sleep bad. Me nerves.

JOAN. Couple of days off and you'll be right as rain.

SANDRA. What's the matter with me? Am I poorly?

JOAN. Aye. But you've got a good nurse for this. I've put your boiler on, the water's hotting up. I'll bring your bath through here. You'll be more comfy.

SANDRA. I feel sick.

JOAN. You're going to have to be sick, good and proper, duck. Sick like you've never been. Sick till your stomach throbs with the pain of it.

SANDRA. I've got to lose it, have I?

JOAN. Yes.

SANDRA. I lost the other one, you know.

JOAN. I know.

SANDRA. I have to write a letter. I have to tell him.

JOAN. Tell him? What the hell do you want to tell him for?

SANDRA. I've got to tell him something very important. Tell him to vote Labour.

JOAN. It's a bit late now.

SANDRA. Is it a bit late now?

JOAN. Keep drinking, duck. (*She fills her glass.*) It's the booze or some horrible herb tablets. The gin's better I tell you. I'll bring the bath through.

JOAN *goes.*

SANDRA. I need to get to bed.

SANDRA *begins, drunkenly, but carefully to take off her clothes, and fold them on a chair.* JOAN *returns with a small zinc bath, which she places on the hearth.*

JOAN. You don't need to take them all off if you don't want.

SANDRA. I'm off to bed. Sleep. Get a good kip.

JOAN. Have a nice bath first. Make you feel better.

SANDRA. Yes, a nice bath.

SANDRA *continues undressing, as* JOAN *comes in from the kitchen a couple of times with a bucket of hot water. Eventually –*

JOAN. That's more than your regulation five inches.

SANDRA. That's naughty.

She begins to giggle, like a schoolgirl.

Honest, you aren't half naughty, Joan. What if they find out?

JOAN. Who's to tell 'em?

SANDRA. Bad girl.

JOAN. That should be hot enough. In you go, our kid. Come on. Take your glass with you.

SANDRA. I don't want a bath. I'll sulk.

JOAN. Mardy, mardy mustard –

SANDRA. Can't eat me custard. Haven't played games in ages.

JOAN. You must have been playing one or two.

SANDRA, laughing, steps into the bath, helped by JOAN.

SANDRA. Where's me soap. (*Furiously.*) Be glad when this fucking war's over. No fucking soap. All right for the dirty boggers. Oh god, it's hot. Redhot. Sweat. Feel the sweat.

JOAN. Oh come on love, sit down. Please.

SANDRA. It's burning me. I'm burning up, Joan. Inside as well. You're burning me.

JOAN. Let go of me Sandra, and I'll go and get some cold water. But it has to be hot, luv, it has to be. I'm sorry. I wish it was otherwise. Can you –

SANDRA. S'all right. If you say hot. Hot.

She almost falls back into the bath.

JOAN. Christ!

She hurries through to the scullery.

SANDRA. I have to write a letter. Dear Albert. Albert. It's ever so hot in England at the moment. (*Laughs.*) I can't sleep at night. Windows wide open. I love you. Nightmares. Pauline I hear her . . . you . . . me crying. Reach out and nails scrape the thin wall, and I go cold, I think I'll rip it, claw it down, so much paper, and I see there's no room there, no bedroom, a wood, a baby crying far away. I think it's Japan. Just the other side of that wall. Like if you dug a hole from Australia you'd fall through to here. Albert I'll catch you. I've caught. Albert. Albert. Don't come, you'll be sick. I'll nurse you. I hate you.

Don't come.

She falls asleep. JOAN *returns, and, kneeling, looks at her.*

JOAN (*tenderly*). You're wasting my precious gin, love. It'll have to be the horse tablets for you. Wake up.

SANDRA. I'm asleep, I've got my eyes closed. Who is it?

JOAN (*imitating ITMA*). It's that man again.

SANDRA. I'm not in.

JOAN. 'Can I do you now, sir?'

SANDRA *laughs.*

JOAN. Popping next door again, love. Don't worry.

SANDRA *starts to sing 'Sailing Down the River on a Sunday Afternoon', quickly getting locked into repeating only 'The Sunday Afternoon'. She occasionally amuses herself by splashing the water.*

BETTY (*voice*). Sandra?

SANDRA. Who is it?

BETTY (*entering*). It's me, love. Joan said you'd got one of your heads again, and not to come in, but I heard you singing –

SANDRA. The wall's so thin.

BETTY. Oh, you're having a bath. I'll leave you be.

SANDRA. It doesn't matter. Come in.

BETTY. Is it bothering your eyes?

SANDRA. What?

BETTY. With the curtains drawn and everything.

SANDRA. Hmm.

BETTY. Joan's gone to get you some aspirins. Look, I won't stay a minute. I just had to tell you. I can't keep it to meself any more. You'll never credit it. You'll never credit what's happened to me. I've met him. I've met that man you saw in the tea-leaves. I know it's crazy but I have. He's a Polish officer, and I met him at a dance, and he's everything you said. Tall, dark and picture-book handsome. And not only that. He's got a castle, well, not a castle, but a big family estate. The Nazis overran it, but now he's just waiting for things to sort themselves out, and away he goes. And he gave me this photo. See, it's got water round it! Amazing, isn't it? Water. I ran all the way to tell you. You were right, it's a new world, you know. Anything can happen. Isn't that fantastic? Honestly, with the water an' all. I had to tell you first.

SANDRA (*stares at photo*). It's all going to come out all right, isn't it?

BETTY (*kneeling by her*). Of course. Here let me pop your water down.

SANDRA. Just bad dreams. Is that all it is?

BETTY. What's in this glass, Sand? What's going on?

SANDRA. Bad dreams.

JOAN *enters*.

JOAN. I told you to stay out.

BETTY. Joan, what's goin' on?

JOAN. Trust you to stick your nose in it. What do you think's going on? Sandra's blind drunk, and sweating in a bath, and I'm bringing her tablets to make her sick. What do *you* think?

A knock at the back door.

JOAN. Bloody hell fire.

She goes. BETTY *stands by the door.* SANDRA *slithers round in the bath to watch her. They look at each other.*

JOAN'S VOICE. What do you want, Johnny?

JOHNNY'S VOICE. Oh, hello, Mrs Stephens. Is Sandra in?

JOAN'S VOICE. Sandra?

JOHNNY'S VOICE. Mrs Downes.

JOAN'S VOICE. She can't come out to play right now, Johnny.

JOHNNY'S VOICE. No, you see, she said she'd vote for me. Vote

Labour. I don't have a vote, you see. Said she'd vote for me.
Said to come round and pick her up.

JOAN'S VOICE. Well, you're out of luck. Sorry.

JOHNNY'S VOICE. Should I call back?

JOAN'S VOICE. She's poorly.

JOHNNY'S VOICE. I'm sorry.

JOAN'S VOICE. Get along with you, lad. I'm busy.

SANDRA. Wait!

Silence.

JOAN'S VOICE. Don't come in.

JOHNNY'S VOICE. Oh, I woun't do that.

JOAN *enters the room.* SANDRA *is rising, drunk, comic, beautiful, from the bath. Her two sisters move forward to help her.*

BETTY. Here –

SANDRA. Don't touch me! Don't . . . nobody . . . touch me!

JOAN. Sandra, love, you're making a big mistake.

SANDRA. What do you think, Betty?

BETTY. How could you, Joan?

JOAN. Don't paint me the black. I'm not the black.

SANDRA. A new world, isn't there? (*She dries herself on the blanket.*)

BETTY. I'll get you a towel.

SANDRA. I'm getting a new one, you know. Got it laid up, special.

JOAN. Leave her.

SANDRA. Nearly got it wrong, me and you, Joan. Bad dreams. Nearly got it dead wrong.

JOAN. I'll not do ought else for you. Putting me in the black.

SANDRA (*putting on underwear, always in danger of falling over*).
They knew, Betty and Johnny.

BETTY. You shoun't go out now, Sand.

SANDRA. Is the sun still out?

BETTY. Yes.

SANDRA. Dry me off. In no time. (*Puts on her dress.*) Nearly set
up. (*Looks for her shoes.*) Where's me shoes? For I have no
stockings to put on. (*Singing.*) Oh, no, John, no, John, no, John,
no.

BETTY. Here they are.

She passes SANDRA *the shoes, and gives her a swift kiss.*

SANDRA. Daft. Don't look so glum, Joan. The sun's shining
through.

She goes out.

JOAN. Don't look like that at me. I'm not the black. You'll see
that when you learn someat of the world.

BETTY. You're wrong. Things are different.

JOAN. Oh, aye. Course you know.

BETTY. I have to be off. I have to meet . . . somebody.

JOAN. Yes.

BETTY *goes out.*

JOAN (*calling out*). You're touched. Both of you.

She contemplates emptying the bath, as the lights fade.

RECORDING. VERA LYNN *singing 'Wishing Will Make it So'.*

Blackout.

Scene Five

A hotel kitchen. Dark stage.

RECORDING. ANNOUNCER. Here is the news. Mr Churchill has resigned. He drove from 10 Downing Street to Buckingham Palace at 7pm tonight. The King accepted his resignation. Labour will have a majority of over 130 seats over all parties in the new House of Commons. The Conservatives have lost nearly 200 seats in their biggest defeat since 1906. The Liberals have been reduced to 10 out of about 300 candidates in the field.

PROJECTION: Day 80. July 26. Labour victory.

CHEF. Off with their heads!

Sudden light. White. SANDRA and MARY stand, cleavers poised over two chickens, awaiting the instructions of HARRY, the CHEF. They all wear white.

CHEF. Now!

They chop off the heads of the chickens.

CHEF. C'est bon, mes petits choux. C'es très bon.

SANDRA *clutches her mouth, in silent mirth.*

Blackout.

RECORDING. ANNOUNCER. Ladies and gentleman, welcome to your own special show, Workers' Playtime.

Signature tune.

Lights up. The CHEF is sitting at the end of the table as the two women draw the fowls.

CHEF (*chuckling*). Stuff the little darlings. Put the wind up their croups. They never saw that one coming did they? Next stop, revolution, brothers. Then, Chicken Kiev for us, the workers!

MARY. If it does come –

CHEF. When it comes –

MARY. If it comes, you'll never get us to eat all that foreign muck. Olive oil and garlic. All that grease.

CHEF. All part of the re-education of the working classes, brother. You wait and see. We'll teach you the joy of the bonne cuisine.

MARY. Cod and chips twice please.

SANDRA. And mushy peas.

CHEF. You cut me to the quick, brothers. Well, you'll get what's coming to you. Top of the list for compulsory spaghetti.

SANDRA. I'd rather do wi' out.

MARY. It makes them I-ties so greasy, they're in and out of beds like ferrets.Coun't do with that sort of going on down Hardstaff Road.

CHEF. Coun't you?

MARY. Not at my time of life.

CHEF. You see, that's your trouble.You're not open to change, you don't really want to be free. You're quite happy plodding along, letting the pigs live off the fat of the land. But that's all over. This is the start of the end for that crowd. Russia liberated all East Europe and it won't be long here now. First off, nationalise the works. No private ownership of houses and all them snobs will be exiled to Skeggie. And every day as a punishment, they'll have to walk out and try and find the sea. A little celebration.

He opens the sherry, pours them a small glass.

SANDRA. How come you've stood working for them so long?

CHEF. Good question, brother. How have I put up with the fact that these officers can fly about, knocking chickens from the skies, while you and me go hungry. Well it an't been easy but you have to see the way things are going. Historical perspective. And historical perspective says they're on their way out. Now I'm a soft-hearted sod, as you well know, and when I think of them poor little rich folk huddled over the candles in the condemned cell next door, me heart bleeds a bit, an' I don't begrudge 'em their last meal. Sides which, I've been slowly poisoning the buggers for years!

MARY. Get away wi' you. (*They laugh.*)

CHEF. True! Slipping in a few toadstools here, and little slivers of Death Caps, in white sauce.

SANDRA. You're having us on!

CHEF. No. Get 'em from ur Colwick Woods. Sunday bus out to Clifton. All over the place. Just slowly rotting their guts for them. Food poisoning. Stomach disorders. Weaken 'em for when the time comes.

MARY. They'll come and take you away one of these days you know.

CHEF. They'll have to prove it first.

MARY. I don't mean the boys in blue. I mean the boys in white. You're off your head.

CHEF. It's them who'll be off their heads. Look, serious for a sec. We've all lost someat. My lad went down at Arnhem 'cos Monty and the Yanks were playing KING OF THE CASTLE. Well, we can't have that no more. The workers can't eat the bread they're getting, cos it's like concrete, so they'll damn well have to go and take the cake. And this election shows, without a doubt, the overwhelming desire of the British people to free themselves from the sleep of Capitalism.

MARY. By Christ, Harry, that's a bit of a mouthful.

CHEF. We can't return to what it was. Do you want to end up in the poorhouse?

MARY. I've got a bit put by.

CHEF. You'll have to have more than a bit to end up sunning yourself in Brighton. You're due for someat. You should get old wi' dignity, not stuck out the back with the dustbins.

MARY. Aye, there's that about it.

CHEF. And it in't much to ask.

MARY. No, it in't.

CHEF. But they'll not give it to us. Remember after the first war – coming back, big posters everywhere, HOMES FIT FOR HEROES.

MARY. Aye.

CHEF. Well, we'll learn our lesson this time. We'll not be cheated. We'll have the full works, with no backsliding.

SANDRA. As long as there's no more violence. We've had enough.

CHEF. You figure they'll give it to us with a kiss and a wave. Wish us luck as they wave us goodbye. You can't cook the Christmas bird without getting blood on your hands.

SANDRA. I don't know about that, but –

CHEF. I'm a cook, I know. The only way to keep your hands clean is to get somebody else to blood it for you.

MARY. Calm down, Harry.

CHEF. I'm just trying to explain to the girl.

MARY. No need to bully.

SANDRA. It's all right.

CHEF. You're worse than me wife. And that says someat.

He takes himself off to the other side of the room.

MARY. Don't sulk, Harry! Take no notice of him. He gets carried away with himself, but really he's as soft as sugar. (*Louder.*) And just as sweet.

SANDRA. No more blood, that's all.

MARY. Right. No more blood. Here, doing this chicken don't upset you does, it?

SANDRA *begins to laugh.*

MARY. I meant – you know – with you . . . What did I say? (*She begins to laugh.*)

CHEF (*returning with the bottle again*). Have I missed a good one?

MARY. I don't know what I said (*Laughing.*)

CHEF *begins to laugh. Pours them another round. The laughter slowly subsides.*

CHEF. Daft buggers, aren't we? Here. For a toast. I give you the future. A new world.

MARY and SANDRA. New world.

They drink.

SANDRA (*looking at her overall*). Look at me. First couple of days here and I've marked this already. Honest, I've been trying to keep it clean.

CHEF. That's what you wear it for. To take the muck.

SANDRA. I'll take it home and wash it.

CHEF. Well . . .

They resume work. Eventually –

SANDRA. What you were saying, Harry – about a new world?

MARY. Let it rest now, luv.

SANDRA. No, but I just wanted to say how I mean.

She talks while nervously cutting up the chicken.

SANDRA. I just wanted to say I agreed with you. In a lot of ways. I mean you'd have to be blind not to see. There's the United Nations just set up, and we'll soon beat Japan, and we beat Hitler, when everybody said we had no chance. And after all that evil, good's bound to come. Like in a Holy War. It was dirty and you had to make sacrifices but you knew you were fighting for good and that good would win out. And we'll beat the Japs, fair and square, and then we'll begin again, and build something beautiful. Clean. Jerusalem.

CHEF. You mean we had God on our side?

SANDRA. It doesn't make sense otherwise. I mean, it makes no sense if we fought evil not to have good come out of it. If we do evil ourselves. I mean, that would be a bad joke, and the whole world would pay for that bad joke. Make everything a nightmare from which there was no waking up. I just can't make sense of that otherwise.

MARY (*quietly*). Steady with the knife, duck.

She takes it off her, and places it on the table.

SANDRA. I finished this. Can I go and wash me hands?

CHEF. Course you can.

SANDRA *goes.*

When's her husband coming home?

MARY. Sometime in the autumn, she reckons.

CHEF. Be about due then, won't it?

MARY. Should be.

CHEF. Nice girl. Highly strung.

MARY. Just the sort who catches. No justice. Some go with hundreds, and never catch a cold, she goes with one, and that's that.

CHEF. How's he going to take it?

MARY. How would you take it?

Silence.

CHEF. Losing that first one hit her bad, did it?

MARY. Smashing little fellow he was. Cheeky with it, but sharp as a knife. Just shoot off though. You couldn't keep hold of him. Hit by a car in the blackout, and that was that. Took it bad as you'd expect.

CHEF. Here. (*Indicating the return of* SANDRA.) Nice work this, Sandra. You're coming on. You know, having two speedy workers is too much for me. I'll start putting on weight and living a life of ease, and then where will I be? You'd better knock off early, the pair of you and leave me someat to do.

MARY. Come on, Sandra, me and you'll go and find ourselves a nice queue to stand in.

SANDRA. Sounds lovely.

CHEF. Pass us that knife over, someone.

SANDRA. Here y'are.

CHEF. Ta.

MARY. Let's get off before Stalin changes his mind.

CHEF. Better take these with you. (*He has cut off two pieces of chicken.*) Wrap 'em up. Pop 'em in your bag.

MARY. That'll be welcome.

SANDRA. Not for me, thank you.

CHEF. How do you mean, not for you?

SANDRA. No, thank you.

MARY. Come on, Sandra. a bit of chicken will do you the world of good. She hasn't had a decent meal since the war started to my certain knowledge. Gives her rations away to her sister.

SANDRA. She's got a growing kid.

MARY. Well, you've got a growing kid, in you. Don't be daft.

CHEF. Perks of the trade. That's all.

SANDRA. No. You see, if it's a new age, you've got to start how you mean to go on. You can't slide back. I know it sounds funny, but that's how I feel.

CHEF. Re-allocation of wealth.

SANDRA. Honest, I couldn't.

CHEF. Suit yourself. Plenty of others who will.

SANDRA. I'll see you outside, Mary.

MARY. Shan't be a sec.

SANDRA. 'Night. (*She goes.*)

MARY. Nice of you, Harry.

CHEF. I didn't upset her, did I?

MARY. Don't think so.

CHEF. I din't mean to.

MARY. No.

CHEF. Just trying to help out.

MARY. Yes.

CHEF. Take it. She might change her mind.

MARY. Not her. She's proud, that one, I'll take mine, though. See you, Harry. (*She starts to go.*)

CHEF. Eh!

MARY. Wha'?

CHEF. How about letting your old man out for a celebration drink tonight?

MARY. Don't know about that.

CHEF. Go on. I'll make a quick 'un down the Dale, if I get these desserts done sharp. (*He begins mixing.*)

MARY. I'll see.

CHEF. Gerroff.

MARY. Ta-ra.

CHEF. Eh! (*Laughing.*) Just make sure those buggers get their just desserts, eh?

She leaves. The CHEF *pretends to sprinkle poison in the dessert. He laughs.*

Light fades.

RECORDING. ANNOUNCER. This is the BBC Home Service. At this moment, in London, Washington, Moscow and Berlin, the text of the joint communiqué of the Potsdam Conference, which ended in the early hours of this morning, becomes available for publication. It's a document of some 6,000 words issued over the signatures of Generalissimo Stalin, President Truman, and the Prime Minister Mr Atlee. The three governments reaffirm their intention to bring major war criminals to swift and sure justice.

Blackout.

Scene Six

SANDRA's *living room.*

Early evening. JOAN *stands by the door to the scullery.* BETTY *sits on the settee. Their mother sits, upright, in a chair by the side of the table.*

Silence.

SANDRA *can be heard saying 'goodnight' to* MARY.

JOAN. She's here.

MAM. I have ears.

SANDRA *is whistling 'Wishing will make it so'.*

JOAN. I'll let her know.

MAM. She'll find out soon enough.

BETTY. Do I have to stay, mother?

MAM. Yes.

In the scullery, SANDRA *has stopped whistling. Silence.*

MAM. Through here, Sandra.

SANDRA *enters, tentatively.*

SANDRA. Hello, mam.

MAM. Sandra.

SANDRA. Family gathering. That's nice. (*Smiling.*) Party, is it?

JOAN. What?

SANDRA. You all look so cheerful.

MAM. There's nought here to be laughing at.

SANDRA. Ah.

JOAN. She had to know sooner or later.

MAM. Who's *she* when she's at home?

JOAN. Now then mam.

SANDRA. I were goin' to tell you.

MAM. Aye. Last after the whole bloody street.

Silence.

SANDRA. Just got me butter ration. I'll go stick it in the larder, fore it melts in me bag. It gets hotter. Shan't be a tick.

She goes.

BETTY. Go easy on her, mam.

MAM. Don't go interfering.

BETTY. She's had a bad time. I don't see we should make it any worse.

MAM. You're getting a bit above yourself, m'lady.

SANDRA (*returning*). We were dripping in that kitchen today. Pouring off us it was. Not too dark for you? I keep the curtains closed. Cools it down a bit. Be hell of a Bank Holiday if it goes on like this. (*Sits near* BETTY.) You haven't been round much, Betty. Still going out with that prince of yours?

BETTY. Steady.

SANDRA. That'll be why I haven't seen much of you. (*Suddenly.*) Does Betty have to be here? I'm sure she could find better ways of –

MAM. She's your sister.

SANDRA (*to* BETTY). No offence, luv. I just thought you might fancy bein' off with your bloke.

MAM. She stays. She's family.

SANDRA (*angrily*). Don't talk to me about family.

JOAN. Sandra!

MAM. What do you mean?

SANDRA. Nothing.

MAM. I don't know what accusations you're trying to make against me, Sandra. I had the three of you to bring up, on me own.

SANDRA. Yes. yes. I feel so sticky. I have to come home every night and have a full wash down.

JOAN. Can we get it over with?

MAM. Joan says you mean to go through with it.

SANDRA. Yes.

MAM. And what you going to do with it?

SANDRA. Have it. I'm going to have it.

MAM. Are you going to keep it?

SANDRA. Mam, I sometimes – how can you ask me a question like that? It's not a pet, a puppy, it's a child I'm having like Joan was, or Betty, or me. A kid.

MAM. And what about Albert?

SANDRA. What about him?

MAM. You always were selfish. Stubborn.

JOAN. Now, mam, that's not fair. Sandra'd –

MAM. Wilful. Not like Joan, mardy little kid, had to keep picking her up, putting her down. You looked as though butter woun't melt in your mouth, but you took what you wanted in your quiet way and were as stubborn as a mule.

SANDRA. You put me out of mind when me dad died.

MAM. I had two others to look after.

SANDRA. I reminded you.

MAM. I'll not have that. (*Raises her hand.*) I'll slap you down, my gal.

Silence.

SANDRA. You never gave me a thought.

MAM. Did you give Albert a thought when you went off gallivanting?

SANDRA. Did you give dad a thought? When you were wi' our 'uncle'?

MAM. Don't bandy words with me, my girl. Don't bandy words.

Silence.

SANDRA. Have you got a fag, Joan?

JOAN. Here you are.

SANDRA. First we've spoke in three weeks 'cos of it. We're family, we're all together. I'm sure we mean well to each other. Can't we all get on together? (*Pause.*) Betty?

BETTY. Yes, Sandra.

SANDRA. I'm a bit bushed, luv. Will you pop kettle on? I managed to pick up a packet of tea on the way home, so we'll celebrate. Get the best tea service out.

BETTY. Good idea. (*She goes into the kitchen.*)

MAM. What exactly are we celebrating?

SANDRA. I'm going to have a child. The world is starting anew. That'll do for openers.

JOAN. Listen, mam, if Sandra's set on having it, I don't see we can do much else but back her.

SANDRA *kicks off her shoes, closes her eyes.*

SANDRA. These shoes. What I wouldn't give for a decent pair of shoes. I dream about 'em at night.

MAM. I want my children to be happy. But this is no way. I know. Why do you want to follow in my footsteps?

SANDRA. It in't like that, mam.

MAM. I want to understand. Did you think Albert won't be coming back?

JOAN. Of course she did. She was lonely, that's all. Same as you wi' Uncle.

SANDRA. I knew he would come back.

JOAN. How could you have known? He's been missing for two years.

SANDRA. I knew. (*She stands.*) I'll put me best table cloth out.

She puts up the round table with JOAN's *help, puts out a lace-edged table cloth and best cups and saucers from the sideboard, during the next section.*

MAM (*quietly*). Think of what it will be like for him.

SANDRA. He'll have to get used to it. You'll have to get used to it. And I'm going to have to get used to it. The world's changing. It's not going back to the way it was. I'm not going to go through all that pain and shame you must have gone through. I'm not going to have to keep such a tight rein. It's no way to go destroying things just to forget – to pretend that they're not there. I've caught and I'm going to give birth to the future and I'm going to bear it and tend it and care for it and bring something whole and lovely and alive into the world. And there you are.But if you feel you can't help with the new world, mam, then do us a favour – don't hinder.

JOAN (*stepping in*). Where did you get these cups?

MAM. I'll go home.

JOAN. Stay, luv.

SANDRA. Down the market. Second hand. Not a mark on 'em. Nice, aren't they?

JOAN. Lovely.

BETTY (*enters*). Tea up!

SANDRA. We'll have it all with grace and style. In Japan they have a special tea ceremony that takes hours for drinking tea, they give it out ever so careful.

JOAN. And get stone-cold tea.

BETTY. Have you seen the paper today?

SANDRA. An't had time to glance at it.

BETTY. They were saying that the Jap soldiers were jumping off cliffs in their hundreds, rather than surrendering. Hari-kiri.

JOAN. Like them little rats that run into the sea.

SANDRA. But why would they kill themselves? I mean, the war'll be over soon. All they've got to do is surrender.

BETTY. Probably scared stiff of being took prisoner, seeing what they did to our lads. Scared we'll take revenge on them.

JOAN. We should as well.

SANDRA. Revenge is no good. That would make us as bad as them.

BETTY. Should I pour?

SANDRA. I'll pour. I'll be mother. Come on, mam, gi's a smile. It might never happen. Whatever it is.

MAM. Who's the father of your child, Sandra?

Silence.

JOAN. It doesn't matter mam, honest, it don't.

BETTY. Sandra's not going to desert Albert, are you?

SANDRA. I'll stand by Albert.

JOAN. There you are. See. Albert'll have his fit when he gets back, and then it'll all blow over. It won't be the only case around here, not by a long chalk. It'll all blow over.

MAM. You'll not tell us then?

SANDRA. Nobody needs to know.

MAM. Will you tell Albert, or don't he warrant the right, either?

SANDRA. I'll not tell him. It's not his business.

MAM. You'll just let him go on wondering if it was one of his mates. That'll be a good start for your new world, that will.

SANDRA (*unsteadily pouring the tea*). It's not one of his mates.

MAM. We know.

SANDRA. How do you mean you know? You can't know.

JOAN. We know, Sandra. He admitted it.

SANDRA. Don't be daft. What are you talking about?

MAM. Joan.

JOAN. It won't be hard to figure it out. I live next door. I hardly see you talk to a soul, never mind go out with anybody.

SANDRA. Come on. What . . . what is it you have figured out?

JOAN. I asked him. Point blank. He didn't try to deny it. In fact, he almost boasted about it.

SANDRA. Who did? Who?

JOAN. Johnny.

SANDRA. Johnny. (*She bursts into almost hysterical laughter.*) What do you take me for? He's only a kid.

MAM. The kid's old enough to fight for his country.

SANDRA. You're having me on. I mean he's only hung around here, so that he might catch sight of our Betty. We talked politics, once or twice, that's all. Nothing else.

MAM. Why would he say the child was his, if it wasn't?

SANDRA. I don't know. He's a strange lad. I don't know.

MAM. Come down off your cloud, Sandra, and think of somebody else. When your Albert comes back and finds it were Johnny, you know what he'll do to him, don't you? You know Albert's temper.

SANDRA. It wasn't Johnny. It wasn't anybody from round here. It wasn't anybody Albert has a chance in a million of ever seeing.

MAM. Then who was it then?

SANDRA. It was an I-tie.

BETTY. An I-tie? From up the camp?

SANDRA. Yes.

JOAN. You queued up for one of them POWs?

SANDRA. Yes. (*Quietly.*) I went up there of a Sunday. I queued. I waited outside the gates, until they were let out for the afternoon. I queued. Yes.

BETTY. With all those old women?

SANDRA. I took a picnic. What I could scrape together.

MAM. You're not right, Sandra.

SANDRA. It wasn't Johnny. I don't know why he says that. I
don't want to talk about it anymore.

MAM. You don't want to talk about it anymore. That's fine.
They'd shave your head in France, and worse. Aye and worse. It
had been better for you if it had been Johnny. Better for all of
us.

SANDRA (*quietly*). Your tea's getting cold.

MAM. You're not even guilty are you? No shame? Just leave your
shame to us who've practice. I've done with you.

BETTY. I'll come with you, mam.

MAM. You'll get no help from me.

BETTY *and* MAM *leave.*

JOAN. Say something. (*Pause.*) I'm no angel, but . . .

SANDRA *remains silent.* JOAN *picks up her coat from the back of
the settee, and leaves.*

SANDRA (*with hands around her cup*). Stone cold.

Blackout.

*Overhead spot, lighting the table, with a white cloth, and
SANDRA, still sitting at the table.*

SANDRA. I took a picnic. What I could scrape together. Bread.
My ration of cheese. Flask of tea. I took it all nice. Lace
tablecloth. I stood, looking through the barbed wire. I walked
off when they came out. Bent shouldered men in a crisp March.
March. March. I marched off at a good pace. He was right
behind me. Perhaps he spoke. I don't know. I had to find a
certain place, that I must have found before, but I was still
surprised when we came upon it. I must have found it earlier,
but I couldn't believe it was there, that I had looked for it, that I
was returning to this place. I thought the ground is hard and

dry. It won't stain my tablecloth, won't stain my dress. This is
fine, anything can happen here, in the lace of these trees, and it
won't stain. I knelt, and began to unpack my bag. I knew I
could walk away and it may never have happened. I laid out the
lace cloth, wiped out the creases, set out the flask, the food,
around the edges like for a child's party. I stood and walked
carefully around the outside of the edge. I looked up. I faced
him. We stood apart. It suddenly was a very hot day. I felt faint.
I thought, I'll fall. Look at him, I thought, look at him. He
began to speak. His voice rose. Anger? Hate? I couldn't
understand what he was saying. The crispness was going. The
fog was setting in. His voice grew louder. He was undoing his
clothing. His trousers. I knew what he was saying. He was
giving me orders. He was . . . giving me . . . orders. I looked at
him, and I knew the lace was there, the food was there. I looked
at him. I waited. Slowly his voice faded away. He stood there,
unbuttoned, sad, clumsy against the lace, like a puppet with the
strings broken. I spoke. I think they were the first words I
spoke, and the last bar one. You – I pointed to him –
PRISONER. He looked away. Frowned. Frowned like a little
child. He understood me. It hurt me. NO. I said. I shook my
head, meaning no. He looked up. I crossed the white to him. I
put out my hand to him. I reached into his crumpled clothes, I
touched him. Touched. I felt the shiver. The pulse. He is real. I
. . . he . . . we are both here. The roughness of his clothes, the
softness of the man's skin. I want to go down in front of him. I
want him to go down in front of me. I want things I've never
dreamed of, sins I have always feared. I pray. A second's prayer.
Not to ask, Lord, but to thank. I want to be free, and I am free.
I am real. I am alive. The Lord is my shepherd. I shall not
want. He maketh me to lie down in green pastures: he leadeth
me beside the still waters. Thou preparest a table before me in
the presence of thine enemies; my cup runneth over. Lord. Holy
mother. Holy child. The Rainbow. The Rainbow.

Blackout.

RECORDING. ANNOUNCER. Scientists, both British and
American, have made the atomic bomb at last. The first one was
dropped on Japan this morning. It was designed for detonation

equal to 20,000 tons of high explosives, that's 2,000 times the power of one of the RAF's ten-ton bombs of orthodox design.

Sound of explosion.

Lights slowly up on –

Scene Seven

A place in the woods.

PROJECTION: Day 91. August 6. Hiroshima. Evening.

Early evening. Red sky. Sun's long shadow throws the trees, lace-style, onto the ground.

SANDRA *is laying out the lace tablecloth and flask, cups around the edges. She looks up. A man approaches, and stands over her. It is* JOHNNY. *Long silence.*

SANDRA. Why do you follow me up here?

JOHNNY. I was worried for you.

SANDRA. Go away.

JOHNNY. They've dropped a big bomb on Japan. Won't be long now, they say, all be over.

SANDRA. They've ripped the walls away. Thin enough, anyway.

JOHNNY. Why do you come here?

SANDRA. Looking for food. Mushrooms. Mice. Squirrels. Taking to the woods. The jungles.

JOHNNY. Are you all right?

SANDRA *laughs. Silence.*

We made it then, eh? Labour.

SANDRA. Labour.

JOHNNY. New world. You don't have a cigarette, do you?

SANDRA. No.

JOHNNY. I've ran out. Can't really afford it.

SANDRA. Why?

JOHNNY. Why what?

SANDRA. Why did you say you were the father of my child?

JOHNNY. Well, I was, in a way.

SANDRA. Clear with me, please.

JOHNNY. I was here. (*Pause.*) I saw.

SANDRA. Saw what? Please, what did you see?

JOHNNY. I saw you. I'd brought some kids up the woods for the day. Get them from under their mam's feet for a couple of hours. I thought it were you walking down the ash-path. Kids playing on monkey-puzzle tree. I followed you. I saw you.

SANDRA. You watched?

JOHNNY. Yes.

SANDRA. Was I alone?

JOHNNY. No. You had a POW with you.

SANDRA. Thank you, Johnny. Thank you, Johnny. (*Reaches out.*) Touch me.

JOHNNY. I . . . There were no kids, Sandra. Made them up. I was on me own. I came to look at the soldiers. Sometimes I follow them. In the woods. They don't see me. One bloke did. He hit me. But I came back.

SANDRA. Soldiers.

JOHNNY. I'm nothing, really, Sandra.

SANDRA. Touch me. Any way. Any way.

JOHNNY. I coun't. I coun't touch anybody. What if I had a fit. I have nightmares about that. I'll say I'm father to your baby if it'll help. Glad to. I'd like to help you.

SANDRA. There in't goin' to be no baby.

JOHNNY. How do you mean?

SANDRA. What I say.There in't no baby. Doctor Henderson. Doctor Henderson told me, I made it up. It won't real.

JOHNNY. I don't understand.

SANDRA (*stands. Very quiet*). The Methodists will save you. You'll neither drink or smoke. You'll meet a girl there. You'll marry, make love as much as proof, take Sunday School kids to Matlock. Paddle on the boating pool. You'll be pretty happy. Pretty unhappy. 'Do not despair, Johnny-Head-in-Air. You'll sleep as sound as Johnny Underground.' Go home, Johnny. (*Laughs.*) Go home (*Angry.*)

He half-runs, half-walks away. She remains.

Blackout.

RECORDING. PRESIDENT TRUMAN. The world will note that the first atomic bomb was dropped on Hiroshima, a military base. That was because we wished the first attack to avoid in so far as possible the killing of civilians, but that attack is also a warning of things to come. If Japan does not surrender, then more bombs will have to be dropped on war industries. Unfortunately, thousands of civilian lives will be lost. I urge Japanese civilians to leave Japanese cities immediately, and save themselves from destruction.

Sound of second bomb explosion.

Slow spot on SANDRA, ironing.

Scene Eight

SANDRA's *living-room.*

PROJECTION. *Day 99. August 14. The eve of peace.*

Midnight. SANDRA is ironing her white dress, standing in her slip. Piles of washing lie around her. She is almost blocked off from the rest of the room by her clothes horse, over which lies the lace tablecloth. JOAN stands watching her.

JOAN. Listen, luv, has it sunk in? The war's over. It's over.

SANDRA. Yes. It's sunk in.

JOAN. Well, what the hell you goin' on with your ironing for, cool as a cucumber? Get your hat and coat, and away we go.

SANDRA. Where?

JOAN. We're taking the kids out, bonfire and then all of us go up top of Colwick Woods and watch the dawn come up. Have a picnic.

SANDRA. Who's all of us?

JOAN. You. Me. Our Pauline. Probably Bridie and her kid. Mary. Betty. Mam. Anybody else who's around.

SANDRA. Mam won't want me.

JOAN. She asked me to come and fetch you.

SANDRA. You said you came straight here.

JOAN. She wants all the family together.

SANDRA. I don't understand.

JOAN. We know, duck. About it not bein' . . . you know.

SANDRA. How can you know?

JOAN. Does it matter?

SANDRA. None of you have been near me. Course it matters. I'm the only one who knows.

JOAN. Dr Henderson made a call round mam's. Last Saturday. To tell her.

SANDRA. Saturday?

JOAN. Listen, Sand, I'd have been round like a shot, you know that. Only she didn't tell us until tonight. I don't think she understood it proper. I mean, a woman of her generation. Difficult to grasp. I'm not sure I make head n'tail of it meself.

SANDRA. It's simple enough. I'm not having a child. I never was having a child. I dreamt it. I wanted it. I imagined it. I imagined it all.

JOAN. But everything was going on in you like as if you were?

SANDRA. Yes.

JOAN. I mean, how can that be?

SANDRA. I dreamt it.

JOAN. And the man?

SANDRA. What?

JOAN. Nothing. Look, if you need a shoulder . . . well, you know –

SANDRA. Yes.

Pause.

JOAN. It's a bloody funny time to be doing the ironing.

SANDRA. Just wanted to get it out of the way.

JOAN. You'll come, won't you? I promised mam I'd bring you. She'd be cut up if I didn't.

SANDRA. I can imagine.

JOAN. Get your dress on. I'm itching to be off. Soon be able to go out again, the four of us, eh? Your Albert'll be back and mine'll soon be dancing his way back across the waters. Sing-song. Like the old days (*Sings.*) 'Every time it rains, it rains pennies from Heaven'. I can see him doing that. Couple of pints swaggering up to the stage. Don't half fancy himself, my Charlie. The singing brickie. Mind you, he won't half bad. He won't half bad.

SANDRA *is putting her dress on.* JOAN *has parked herself on the edge of the settee.*

He'll do a quick about turn when he gets home. I've been thinking about it, need to get out of this town. Been like a prison last six years, no trains to go anywhere, no excursions. I'll get him on the move before he falls back with his cronies. Get right away. Down south. Maybe emigrate. Canada, Australia, one of them places. What do you think?

She steps forward automatically to help with SANDRA's *zip.*

SANDRA *stiffens*.

SANDRA. You'll not go anywhere. You'll end up changing his pants for him twice a day, bathing him, turning him over. You both deserve better than that.

JOAN (*shaken*). Steady on there, eh?

SANDRA *looks away*. JOAN *moves hair back from* SANDRA's *face*.

You're looking a bit peaky. Been staying in too much. Get you out in the sun. Soon have you back in the traps, eh?

SANDRA. How's Pauline?

JOAN. She's missed you. I just dragged her out of bed. Tottering around like a drunk, but couldn't let her miss it. Larkin is going to get his piano in the street, and someone's coughed up an old mattress to start the bonfire off. And we're all getting bits of snap ready for the picnic.

SANDRA. I'll get something packed up, should I?

JOAN. That's more like our Sandra.

SANDRA. I've got a few things I've been saving.

JOAN. Well, now's the time to get 'em out. Five minutes, right. And don't lock your door again. There's no need. And there never will be. OK?

SANDRA. No, I won't.

JOAN *goes out*. SANDRA *takes the tablecloth off the horse*.

Blackout.

RECORDING. ATTLEE. Friends, friends, it is now three months ago since we celebrated the defeat of Germany. At that time many of us could not feel as happy as we do tonight because our boys were still fighting in the east. Today, with the defeat of Japan, peace comes again at last throughout the whole world.

Scene Nine

The top of Colwick Woods.

PROJECTION: Day 100. August 15. Victory in Japan Day.

During the recording of General MacArthur, the light slowly begins to rise over an open stage. It takes a long time. The speech can be broken with silence to relate more strongly with the dawn effect.

Throughout the scene, the light slowly builds, draining the 'dry' stage of any colour it might possess.

In the distance can be seen the indistinct form of the camp. MOTHER *enters to down-stage with* MARY. *Towards the end of the speech,* JOAN *enters, with* BRIDIE *pushing a pram.* JOHNNY *walks on.* SANDRA *follows, her bag by her side. They are largely shadows, if that. They all stand and look out over the audience.*

RECORDING. MACARTHUR. Today the guns are silent.
  A great tragedy has ended: a great victory has been won.
  The skies no longer rain death.
  Men everywhere walk upright in the sun.
  The entire world lies quietly at peace.
  The Holy Mission has been completed.

The recording ends. The cast continue looking out over the audience. SANDRA *breaks the spell, first. She tests the ground for damp. She sits, and lays out her thin blanket. She lays her folded tablecloth to one side. She takes out a bread-knife, a small loaf and begins to slice it.*

MAM. Dawn.

MARY. Grand.

MAM. It is that, and no mistake.

BRIDIE. Some of them fires are still going.

MARY. Where?

BRIDIE. Down there, left of the big Boots building.

MARY. Where would that be then?

MAM. Wilford Lane way.

MARY. Would be, ye'.

MAM. See the smoke taking up with the mist from the Trent? Going to be a scorcher again today.

JOAN. It's been a fair while since I've been up with the dawn.

MAM. Our Betty were the last time with me.

BRIDIE. The same with me.

MAM. Funny how babies always hang on till half an hour before dawn, and then . . . (*Fades away.*)

Silence. JOAN *lights up and gives* BRIDIE *one.*

JOAN. She's as good as gold, isn't she?

BRIDIE. It's the fresh air. Knocked her senseless.

JOHNNY. I wish someat'd knock my little bugger senseless, for a couple of hours. Mary?

MARY. Ta. (*She catches the cigarette* JOAN *throws to her.*)

JOAN. You want one, Sand?

SANDRA. No, thank you.

JOAN. Chuck 'em over to chimney pot, Mary. He won't say no.

MARY *throws them.* JOHNNY *misses them. He moves to pick them up. This effectively breaks their set positions.*

JOAN. Brave try, anyhow.

MAM. Look at our Sand. Hard at work.(*Crosses to her.*)

JOHNNY (*returning cigarettes to* JOAN). Ta.

MAM (*kneeling*). I'll give you a hand, luv.

JOAN. Well, I'm standing here, as if I an't got a care in the world, and I an't the foggiest where our Pauline is.

JOHNNY. I gave her a piggy up the hill, but she ran down again to join her mates.

JOAN. Hard done by, aren't you?

JOHNNY. I don't mind.

MAM. I'll butter them for you.

SANDRA. Thanks, I'd prefer to do it myself.

JOAN. I'll go and look for her.

JOHNNY. Shall I help you look?

JOAN. Better stay there, Johnny. I don't want to get side-tracked, into the bushes. (*She goes.*)

MAM. You reckon this ground is really dry?

SANDRA. Bone dry. But you can sit on the blanket if you want.

MAM. Getting grass stains out is such a hell of a job. Milk don't always do it.

BRIDIE (*to* JOHNNY, *who is looking in the pram*). Don't you go waking her up now.

JOHNNY. I wouldn't do that.

BRIDIE. First bit of peace I've had.

She begins to set out her picnic by the pram.

If she wakes up, the whole bloody world'll know about it.

MARY (*still looking on*). You'd think you could see thousands of miles, woun't you? All the way to Australia.

BRIDIE. Nice view of West Bridgford at any rate.

JOHNNY has taken himself up-stage.

MAM. Joan told you then, did she?

SANDRA. Yes.

MAM. Aye, she said she had. Took me a bit of time, to get it sorted out in me mind. I didn't understand him proper, at first.

SANDRA. No.

MAM. What it was you see, was I'd never heard of ought like that before. I was just stunned when he explained it to me. Well, I mean you must have been an' all.

SANDRA. Yes.

MAM. Did you know such things were possible?

SANDRA. No.

MAM. I've always wanted the best for my girls, you know that.

SANDRA. Yes.

MARY (*crossing to* BRIDIE). I'm getting a bit tired now. It fair takes the winds out of your sails. I could do with a week in bed.

BRIDIE. So could I.

MARY. You're getting as bad as your mate.

BRIDIE. I should be so lucky.

MAM. Listen, I know this is going to sound terrible, I mean it's the sort of thing that can send you up the wall when people say it to you but the fact is that it's true and you need to remember that. It will all work out for the best. You coun't have had that kid, anyway, and now you're set up again to start afresh. It's a blessing. It really is. It's God's will. And there's nought folk can do about that. Except go along and see the sense of it.

SANDRA (*holding out bread*). Crust?

MAM. Just a sec. Just a sec. It isn't easy for me, this, but let me get off me chest what I have to say. Now you see, it'll be all right now. You'll see the good coming from it. And all you have to do is put out of your mind this whole nightmare of meeting this bloke and all the rest of it.

SANDRA. You don't think I really met him.

MAM. We might have our ups and downs, but I know me own daughter. I didn't need a doctor to tell me everything. I carried you around long enough. And reluctant enough you were to leave me. Now, let's forget it ever happened, and get down to the slog of real life, eh?

SANDRA. Here you are. I've buttered it for you.

MAM. Right. I'm set to risk me teeth on it. I'm partial to a bit of crust, you know.

SANDRA. I know.

MARY *has walked across to* JOHNNY *who faces up-stage, looking at the camp.*

MARY. Be glad to see the back of that camp. Hideous thing.

JOHNNY. What'll they do with it now they've sent the I-ties home?

BRIDIE (*chirping in*). They should send us all them Japs, and let us gals gi' them some stick. What do you say, Sandra?

SANDRA *looks up, then resumes her work.*

MARY. They've got off lightly. A couple of towns bombed, and it's all over. We took it for six years.

BRIDIE. Funny in't it? You'd think they'd all have done themselves in, the way the soldiers did. Their civvies must be soft – can't stand a blitz or two.

MAM. This is a treat. Nice bit of bread for a change.

MARY. Said in the Post they might use these camps for refugees. But I can't see that. I mean, why would a refugee want to live in one of them? Now the war's over they'll all go home, won't they? All these Poles and Czechs, and what have you. Like Betty's lad. They aren't going to want to stay here when they can go home to their own kind.

JOHNNY. Probably just knock the whole thing down.

MARY. High time. Used to be a bit of flat land for the lads to kick a ball about on.

BRIDIE. Did you read that thing in the Post last night?

MARY. What, about the bombs?

BRIDIE. No. The headline story.

MARY. That Nottingham girl, Vera?

BRIDIE. Rum do, that, you know. They're not givin' us all the facts on that. Eighteen-year-old girl goes all the way to London to stay near a 32-year-old lorry driver, and everybody says it was above board, and then he goes and does her in. No reason.

MARY. It struck me as funny that –

JOAN *enters, with a somewhat bedraggled* PAULINE.

JOAN. I found her. Half way to China. Look at her. She's covered in muck.

MAM. Here. (*Rising.*) Let your gran clean you up a bit. (*Takes out hanky, spits on it.*)

JOAN. I don't know where they find the muck. I reckon there's some little bloke selling it somewhere, like ice cream. Look at your dress.

MAM. You'll not look like a princess for the Procession. Lick and a spit'll make your face shine, at any rate.

JOAN. Leave her, mam. I want her to get a bit of shut-eye.

MARY. It's only once in a lifetime

JOAN. It's been twice this year. Any more Victories, and she's going on parade bare-bummed.

MAM. Let her play.

JOAN. Oh, aye, she'll play all right, she'll play merry hell this afternoon, when she wants to go to the party, and she's all tired out and narky. Oh, go on, then. Go and bury yourself.

PAULINE *rushes off, almost knocking* BETTY *over, as she enters.*

BETTY. Steady.

JOAN. Here comes the sleeping beauty.

SANDRA *who has finished making sandwiches, takes little or no interest in other activities, unless directly addressed.*

MAM. And where have you been, madam?

JOAN. Up to no good I'll be bound.

BETTY. You've no romance in your soul.

JOAN. Food in your belly. That's all you need.

MAM. Come on Betty.

BETTY. I have been dancing round bonfires. Round and round.

MARY. Well, doing the Hokey-Cokey never harmed anybody.

JOAN. Speak for yourself.

BETTY. I've been waltzing.

JOAN. Even worse. You'll have to lock her up, mam.

BETTY. Too late.

MAM. Now don't say things like that, Betty. You make me heart skip a beat.

BETTY. Oh, don't be daft, mam. I didn't mean that. Look. (*She holds out her hand. On her engagement finger is a curtain ring.*)

JOAN. Nail varnish, eh? Painted hussy.

BETTY. No. Don't play games. What do you think?

JOAN. What do you think of it, mam?

MAM. Well, I'm hardly surprised.

BETTY. Catch it with the light on it. See the sun glinting on all the rainbow colours in the diamond. See the bloodred of that ruby begin to throb.

JOAN. Now you say, I do begin to see someat. The green of the emerald is a bit flashy, but look at the blue of that sapphire – like a baby's eyes. Beautiful.

BRIDIE (*laughing*). Must have cost a fortune.

BETTY. See, Mary.

MARY. It's a lovely ring, my dear. You're a very lucky girl to have such a generous fellow. Isn't she Johnny?

JOHNNY. Well, he's a v-v-very lucky fellow an' all.

BETTY. Well, thank you kind sir. See, Sandra.

She crosses to her.

SANDRA. What?

BETTY. See what my Polish airman gave me?

SANDRA. A curtain ring.

BETTY. No, Sandra, come on. Look again. Isn't it the most fantastic engagement ring you've ever seen? With all those diamonds, sapphires, emeralds, rubies . . .

JOAN. It must weigh a ton. Put your hand in the pram, and we'll wheel it home.

BETTY. Well, mam, what do you say?

MAM. Is he going to take you away from us?

JOAN. He'd better. I don't want my sister stuck in this dump all her life.

BRIDIE. He'll fly you away to his castle in the sky.

BETTY. Well, it's not exactly a castle, but it's a big place with lots of land to farm. And animals. Cows and sheep.

BRIDIE. Does he do it all himself?

BETTY. No, he has men working for him.

BRIDIE. Wish he'd asked me.

BETTY. Well, mam?

MAM. You have my blessing, luv. Course you do.

BETTY *kisses her.*

Now, enough of that. I've never gone in for that sort of stuff.

JOAN. It'll work out for you. I feel it. Even if he is a foreigner.

BETTY. They can't help it.

JOAN. I'm not blaming 'em. A duck can't be a swan. I don't blame it. It's just a fact. They have to learn to live with it.

BRIDIE. Listen to Lady Muck.

MARY. Your mam'll miss you.

MAM. The cost of loving is losing.

BETTY. Oh, mam. You'll come for holidays.

MAM. Aye.

BRIDIE. I wish you every happiness.

BETTY. Thank you, Bridie.

MAM. It's all gettin' too much for me. I could do wi' forty winks, 'fore we have breakfast.

MARY. Come on. Let us old ones close our eyes for a minute.

They lie back on their coats.

JOAN. I'll toast your future wi' a cup of tea, seeing as there's nought better.

She kisses BETTY.

BRIDIE. God, what a day! It's going to be a blisterer.

She sits, leaning against the pram, while JOAN *pours the tea.* BETTY *crosses back to* SANDRA; *sees* JOHNNY *who is now sitting upstage, quietly lighting a cigarette.*

BETTY. You all right Johnny?

JOHNNY. Oh yes, fine, Betty, I'm fine.

When he finishes his cigarette, he lies back with his hands behind his head. The light is now getting strong.

JOAN (*sitting by* BRIDIE): You got the handbrake on this?

BRIDIE. Course it has.

JOAN. Wouldn't like to drop off, and wake up to find grooves in me neck.

She sits, sipping her tea, half-dozing.

BETTY. Sandra?

SANDRA. Yes, love.

JOAN (*calling across*). Eh, Betty, did you get rid of them letters?

BETTY. I put them on a bonfire at one this morning. I watched them burn away.

JOAN. Good gal.

BETTY(*quietly, kneeling*). Sandra, this ring was given me by the man you saw in the tea leaves. He's asked me to be his wife, and I'm going back to Poland with him. I wanted you to know.

SANDRA. I can understand you, Betty. Can you understand me?

BETTY. What do you mean?

SANDRA. I have to tell you there is no Poland. I made it up. It's a fairy tale. I dreamt it. Doesn't exist. You will never get there. It doesn't exist. It's a curtain ring. Never be anything else. Do you understand what I'm saying?

BETTY. Sandra, you're hurting my hand.

SANDRA. Sorry.

BETTY *rises.* SANDRA *looks down.*

BETTY. It's so hot. So unbelievably hot. You know what I would like to do? Not that I'd dare, anyway.

SANDRA. No.

BETTY. I could tuck my skirt up though, couldn't I, and get the sun to my leg. So much sun seems a sin not to get a good tan.

SANDRA. A sin.

BETTY. There's only Johnny here, and he doesn't really count. It'll be all right, won't it?

SANDRA. Yes.

BETTY. OK.

She tucks her skirt up. Stands for a moment, reaching up to the sun.

Oh, this is wonderful. What a day. I never dreamt I could have such a day. (*She sits, then lies back*). Eh, Sandra?

SANDRA. Yes.

BETTY. Isn't it fantastic?

SANDRA *watches her.* PAULINE *enters, carrying mushrooms in her skirt. She crosses to her mother.*

SANDRA. Ssssh! What have you got there?

PAULINE. Mushrooms.

SANDRA. Where did you get them?

PAULINE. I found them. Can we have them for breakfast?

SANDRA. Bit tricky to cook them here.

PAULINE. Couldn't we leave them on a hot stone.

SANDRA. Could do. But we don't know if they're poisonous or not?

PAULINE. Are some poisonous?

SANDRA. Lots of them and they look just the same as the good ones, but if you eat them, you begin to swell up, and your skin breaks out into spots, and the sweat pours off you, and you're sick all the time and then eventually you die. So you have to be ever so careful with them.

PAULINE. How do you know if it's poisonous or not?

SANDRA. You eat it and find out.

PAULINE (*laughing*). That's silly.

SANDRA. Of course it's silly. It's one of God's silly jokes. They make him laugh. But they hurt you and me. So you have to be very careful 'cos he's playing tricks like that all the time.

PAULINE. What sort of tricks?

SANDRA. Well, do you remember me telling you about the rainbow, that's one of his tricks. You see, really, he was ever so cunning and he only promised not to flood us all again. So he brings the sun out when it rains and everybody cheers, and he's chuckling away to himself, because he sees what we don't see. He sees that slowly he's drying us out. Drying the skin. Making the waters of life in us rise like mist. And we're still walking around you see, still thinking we're fresh and alive, and we're dead really. There's no water in us. And a few begin to crack first, they crack like glass 'cos they're so dry, and fall into a fine dry dust that blows away in the wind, and nobody can tell they were ever there. Just so much dust in the air. No life in them. And the best part of the joke for God is that we don't even see this. We like to stay in the cities and camps, going through the motions in the dusty air. We don't see he's taking the life from us and replaced it with a dry warmth that –

JOAN. That's enough, Sandra. You're frightening the kid.

PAULINE. I'm not frightened.

JOAN. I say you're frightened, you're bloody frightened. Come over here.

PAULINE. I was listening to Auntie Sandra.

SANDRA. Go on. Go over to your mam, luv.

She goes over to her mother.

JOAN. Now come on, just sit still for five minutes. (*She nestles up by her.*) Don't work it out on the kids, Sandra.

SANDRA *looks at the mushrooms that* PAULINE *had let fall in front of her. She picks one up. She looks around her, at the lying figures.*

Blackout. Short snatch of Yiddish 'Kaddish der Jud is rejodt'. Lights up, as in Scene Seven. The rest of the stage remains dark.

SANDRA *repeats her actions as at the beginning of Scene Seven. She lays out the lace tablecloth, places flask, cups etc. around the edge. She looks up.*

Blackout.

RECORDING (*interwoven and overlapping*).

MACARTHUR. The skies no longer rain death.

DIMBLEBY. You could not see which was except by a convulsive –

MACARTHUR. Men everywhere walk upright in the sun.

DIMBLEBY. The living lay with their heads against the corpses.

MACARTHUR. The entire world lies quietly at peace.

DIMBLEBY. Unable to look at the terrible sights around them.

MACARTHUR. The Holy Mission is completed.

Light up.

SANDRA *lies, face forward, on her cloth. The cups have fallen over.*

The entire stage is now lit. The cast sleep, or lie. An occasional small movement. The lights swiftly build to a white heat – if possible, lights aimed directly on the audience. A sudden intense blinding effect. Swiftly to m—

Blackout.

Stephen Lowe
Touched

1945, the hundred days between victory in Europe
and victory in Japan; in a working-class suburb of
Nottingham, a group of women emerge from the
tight rein of war. A new future beckons with the
impending return of the soldiers.

'Stephen Lowe's **Touched** . . . is a beautifully
written piece effortlessly linking the private and
public worlds.'
Michael Billington, **Guardian**

'**Touched** is truly identified with working people
and a radical vision, unlike many contemporary plays
for which the same claim is made.'
Jim Hiley, **Time Out**

'Excellent'
John Elsom, **Listener**

ISBN 0-413-61210-4

9 780413 612106

PRICE NET
£4.50
IN UK ONLY
A METHUEN PAPERBACK
PLAYS